BRIT

A ONE PARTY STATE?

CHRISTOPHER HELM VITAL ISSUES SERIES
Series Editor: Geoffrey Alderman

BRITAIN
A ONE PARTY STATE?

Geoffrey Alderman

CHRISTOPHER HELM
London

© 1989 Geoffrey Alderman

Christopher Helm (Publishers) Ltd, Imperial House,
21–25 North Street, Bromley, Kent BR1 1SD

ISBN 0–7470–0004–2

A CIP catalogue record for this book
is available from the British Library

Typeset by Florencetype Ltd, Kewstoke, Avon
Printed and bound in Great Britain by Billing and Sons Ltd,
Worcester

Contents

Tables

Preface

Whatever historians will make of the premiership of Margaret Thatcher, and of the Conservative administration she has led since the general election of 1979, we who are living through this administration need to understand how it came about, what it is about, and why it has lasted so long and shows every sign of even greater longevity. I do not claim that I have definitive answers to any of these questions. Neither do I claim to be able to explain the deeper motives (other than a concern for the public good) that lead women and men to enter politics, and to attempt to re-order society and government according to particular sets of ideals. I offer the work which follows merely as a contribution towards our understanding of the political times in which we live, casting a critical but wary eye over the entire face of political activity on mainland Britain.

No political scientist can claim to be 'above politics'. I have tried to be neutral in politics. For the benefit of those who are curious about such matters, I am neither a member nor a supporter of any political party.

I am grateful to Professor Andrew Likierman, of the London Business School, for enlarging my knowledge of certain aspects of British public finance, and to generations of students to whom I have had the pleasure of teaching British politics, whose close questioning has made me define, sharpen and redefine my own views. Richard Wigmore, of Christopher Helm, read through the entire typescript and has saved me from many errors and infelicities. For those which remain I alone am responsible.

Geoffrey Alderman
October 1988

1. 1987

On 11 June 1987 the Conservative Party was returned to power for a third consecutive term; Mrs Thatcher, who had already become the longest-serving Prime Minister since Winston Churchill (and who is now Britain's longest continuous serving Prime Minister this century, and the longest-serving leader of the modern Conservative Party) won her third consecutive general election, a record equalled only by Lord Liverpool (also a Tory) in the early nineteenth century and William Pitt (a Tory in practice) at the end of the eighteenth. In terms of seats, the Conservative victory of 1987 was a landslide, even though the overall majority that emerged was smaller than in 1983. The parliamentary position of the Labour Party improved only marginally compared with 1983, while the number of MPs elected under the SDP–Liberal Alliance banner fell by almost a fifth. Plaid Cymru—the Welsh Nationalist Party—gained one seat, and the Scottish National Party also made a net gain of one.

The scale of the Conservative victory (an overall majority of 100 seats) not only assured Mrs Thatcher of an historic third term in office; it confirmed the apparent inability of the Alliance to break the two-party mould of British politics, and—more importantly—resulted in a Parliamentary Labour Party comprising the second lowest number of Labour MPs since 1945. Excluding the bleak year of 1983, when the proportion of the British electorate voting Labour fell to 27.6 per cent (the lowest post-war percentage), the electoral popularity of the Labour Party was still weaker in 1987 than at any general election since 1931, when Ramsay MacDonald betrayed the party he had helped to establish, and called an election as Prime Minister of a National Government that was, in fact, largely Conservative in composition. In October 1931 Labour entered the electoral contest in a palpably weak and demoralised state, and in a condition of shock; in the circumstances the party did well to obtain 30.6 per cent of votes cast. In June 1987 the party could manage to gain no more than 30.8 per cent of the votes, even though it appeared united, had acquired in Neil Kinnock a forceful and photogenic leader, and, according to popular wisdom, had run a campaign that was more polished and better projected than that of any of its opponents.

Media presentation of election results tends to be highly simplistic, and based on a number of assumptions that are rarely explained to readers, listeners and viewers. In 1983 the term 'landslide' was widely used to describe a Conservative victory that was, indeed, magnificent from the point of view of its parliamentary majority (144 over all other parties); but this result was obtained on a *lower* share of the vote than in 1979 (42.4 per cent compared with 43.4 per cent when Mrs Thatcher first came to power). Moreover, to base the statistical presentation of election outcomes on those who voted ignores the very important phenomenon of rational abstention. If we are to obtain a true measure of popular support for a political party, we need to base our calculations on electors who might have voted rather than on voters who did so.

This differentiation becomes crucially important when we talk about 'swing', a concept that is invariably invoked by the pundits without comment or explanation, even in the quality press. Thus, *The Guardian* of 13 June 1987 declared that in Great Britain there had been a swing 'from Conservative to Labour nationwide' of 2.5 per cent, but did not say whether this calculation rested on those who voted (conventional swing), those who could have voted (electoral swing) or merely (as was in fact the case) upon those who voted Conservative and Labour (two-party swing). Swing itself is of course a statistical abstraction—the averaging of one party's percentage gain or loss against another's; to say that there was a swing of 2.5 per cent from Conservative to Labour does not mean that 2.5 per cent of those who, in total, voted for either of these two parties switched sides, but simply that this was the *net* result of the multiplicity of switching of votes that takes place at an election.

If, for the moment, we employ the term swing to refer to the electorate, not to that proportion of the electorate that voted, we obtain a much sharper picture of the outcome of the 1987 election. Using the figures in Table 1.1 we can see that although the Conservatives suffered a net loss of seats in 1987, their national

Table 1.1 Electoral support for the parties, 1983 and 1987

	1983 (%)	1987 (%)
Conservative	30.8	31.9
Labour	20.0	23.3
Alliance	18.3	17.0
Nationalist	1.1	1.3
Others	2.5	2.0
Did not vote	27.3	24.5

popularity increased somewhat compared with 1983, by a percentage that was matched almost exactly by that lost by the Alliance. Labour support increased by over 3.0 per cent. Overall, there was a national *electoral* swing of 1.0 per cent to Labour. To achieve parity with the Conservatives next time, Labour will need a swing of over four times the size achieved in 1987. In trying to assess whether this is possible, we need to remember that Harold Wilson's 1966 victory was achieved on an electoral swing of only 2.0 per cent, while the 1979 Conservative victory rested on a swing of 3.9 per cent. In conventional terms, confining ourselves to those who would actually vote, the swing would need to be of the order of 8 per cent; not since 1945 has such a result been achieved.[1]

In short, and excluding the possibility of some totally unforeseeable electoral sensation, past performance would indicate that the likelihood of the Conservatives being thrust from office at the next general election is slim indeed. Even if the Conservatives were to lose many votes, the intervention of a third party could well preserve their hold on enough seats to sustain them in office well into the second half of the 1990s. By then, a generation will have grown up that will hardly remember (if it remembers at all) a time when the United Kingdom was governed by any party other than the Conservatives, who will with some justification be able to refer to themselves as the natural party of government.

In a sense, this has already become the case. It was not until 1928 that Britain acquired a reasonably democratic franchise, with the right to vote being given to most men and women of 21 years of age and over, regardless of considerations of wealth and poverty. In the subsequent 60 years, alone or in coalition, the Conservatives have been in office for no less than 41. The Liberals last held office in 1915 (and the last Liberal government to command its own majority in the Commons was that of 1906–10). There have only

Table 1.2 Percentage share of the vote, 1929–1987

	Con	Lab	Lib/ Alliance
1929	38.2	37.1	23.4
1931	55.2	30.6	7.0
1935	53.7	37.9	6.4
1945	39.8	47.8	9.0
1950	43.5	46.1	9.1
1951	48.0	48.8	2.5
1955	49.7	46.4	2.7
1959	49.4	43.8	5.9
1964	43.4	44.1	11.2
1966	41.9	47.9	8.5
1970	46.4	43.0	7.5
1974 (F)	37.9	37.1	19.3
1974 (O)	35.8	39.2	18.3
1979	43.9	37.0	13.8
1983	42.4	27.6	25.4
1987	42.3	30.8	22.6

been two periods of majority Labour rule (1945–51 and 1964–70). The lion's share of the popular vote has, likewise, generally been cast in the Tory interest, as Table 1.2 indicates. Indeed, as the non-Tory vote has become less unevenly divided between Labour and the Alliance at recent general elections, the advantages which the Conservatives derive from the present electoral system have become more marked.

The vagaries of the electoral system will be considered in more detail in due course. Here we must concentrate on voters and issues. How has it come to pass that a mass electorate, and a society that has become more egalitarian, has continued to support Conservative policies and Conservative candidates? Ought we to be surprised that such support has been sustained over so long a period of time?

In attempting to answer these questions we must, inevitably, confront the issue of 'class'. In the nineteenth century Marxists and non-Marxists alike agreed that Britain was a class-based society, divided into an upper, landowning class, an industrial and commercial bourgeoisie, and a class of wage-labourers. But this was a social, not a political, typology. When Victorians voted, their particular *occupation* was likely to play a more influential role than their social position, and religious affiliation also played a major part. Landowners, Anglicans and labourers were more likely to vote Conservative than Liberal, while Dissenters, shopkeepers, craftsmen and businessmen were more likely to vote Liberal than Conservative. The parties led by Gladstone and Disraeli appealed to religious and economic interests within the (all-male) electorate, not to whole classes of society.

In the first half of the twentieth century the occupational basis of voting behaviour gave way—or at least appeared to give way—to a distinct class alignment. The transformation is generally associated with the rise of the Labour Party, which appealed primarily to wage-labourers (especially, though not exclusively, to trade-union-organised wage-labourers), the majority of whom were not enfranchised until the passage of the Representation of the People Act of 1918. Before 1918 only male heads of households were entitled to vote; women could not vote at all in parliamentary elections. This meant that, among the manual working classes, the right to vote tended to be restricted to the skilled artisans, who earned relatively high wages; most of these tended to be of the Liberal persuasion. It was, undoubtedly, the passage of the 1918 Act (which almost trebled the size of the electorate) that made possible the transformation of Labour into a mass party and a party of potential government. As the Liberal Party entered upon its decline in the period 1918 to 1924, those members of the manual working classes who could vote for the first time voted Labour; the more conservative-minded 'Lib-Lab' voters deserted to the Conservative camp.

With the virtual disappearance of Liberalism as a major force in British politics after 1935, the country entered upon a period (1935–70) of genuine two-party politics, each side drawing its electoral strength from well-defined areas of the country: Labour from South Wales, Inner London, the West Midlands, South Yorkshire, Merseyside, North-East England and Mid-Scotland; the Conservatives from Southern England, East Anglia, the agricultural ('shire') counties of the Midlands and the North, and from Northern Ireland, whose Protestant and Unionist majority had historic links with the Conservative Party at Westminster. Within these areas were to be found parliamentary constituencies of reasonably uniform social composition. Those seats in which the social composition was more fluid formed the real electoral battleground.

In this connection it is worth noting that the number of such seats was generally not large. At the election of 1951 that brought to an end the Attlee government, only 28 seats (out of 625) changed hands. But during the 1960s the battleground area became significantly larger. When Labour returned to power in 1964, 70 seats (out of 630) changed hands, and the number rose to 89 when Edward Heath became Prime Minister in 1970; nine years later 72 seats (out of 635) changed hands to give Mrs Thatcher her first election victory. Neither in 1964 nor in 1970 nor in 1979 had boundary changes taken place, so that these outcomes may be considered a real measure of an increasingly volatile electorate.

Other indices point in the same direction, and to the same period of post-war electoral history at which change may be detected. One is the declining share of the vote and of the electorate captured by the Conservative and Labour Parties combined (see Tables 1.1 and 1.2). Throughout the 1950s roughly eight out of ten eligible electors considered it worthwhile to bother to vote; the vast majority of these votes (on average, 94 per cent) went to the Labour and Conservative Parties. But in the 1960s and 1970s turnout fell to an average of 75 per cent. Moreover, the two major parties' share of this declining vote also fell: in 1974 only three-quarters of the voters (less than six out of every ten *electors*) supported the two major parties. In 1983 the combined Conservative and Labour share of the vote fell to just 70 per cent (the lowest post-war proportion), and though it rose to 73 per cent in 1987, this support still amounted to only 55 per cent of the electorate.

To this evidence we may add that provided by the results of by-elections. It is, of course, natural for governments in mid-term to be less popular than they were immediately after the general elections that brought them to power. In the 1950s it was rare for anti-government swings (measured in conventional terms) at by-elections to be above 10 per cent; between 1950 and 1966 there were only nine such cases in 187 contests. But in the parliament of 1966–70 there were 16 in 38 contests, and between the elections of 1983 and 1987 no less than 13 out of 16 fell into this category.[2]

Expert opinion, though agreed that the behaviour of the electorate became much less predictable during and after the late 1960s, is divided as to the causes. A number of theories are worth examining here, especially since they all bear heavily upon the 1987 election result. These explanations are not mutually exclusive.

The first centres upon the crumbling of the relationship between occupational class and political allegiance. It needs to be stressed that even in the period 1935 to 1970 this correlation was never a complete one; if it had been, Labour would have enjoyed much longer periods in office. To obtain some measurement of the relationship, we must rely on survey data collected by the major opinion-research organisations, who traditionally use variations of the six-fold categorisation employed by the Institute of Practitioners in Advertising, as follows:

A   – Professional and higher managerial
B   – Administrative and lower managerial
C1 – Supervisory, clerical and skilled non-manual
C2 – Skilled manual
D   – Semi-skilled and unskilled manual
E   – State pensioners and casual workers

The drawbacks inherent in this method of classification are many. The C1 category includes highly qualified supervisory staff as well as relatively unskilled shop assistants and lodging-house keepers. The assumption that *all* state pensioners have the same sets of political outlooks and social prejudices as casual workers is clearly questionable. The entire categorisation is based on a male-orientated society—an approach that is, perhaps, to some extent legitimate for the period before 1970, but which must clearly be abandoned thereafter. Scarcely less serious is the fact that the division of society into occupational grades (which may be entirely legitimate from the point of view of the advertising industry) presupposes that occupation and income (and, therefore, life-style) are the major determinants of voting behaviour.

This may well have been true of British society in the mid-twentieth century. Voting is a secret act, in which it is possible that many of those who cast votes do so on a basically selfish premiss: which party is most likely to implement policies that will raise *my*, or *my family's,* standard of living? Which party will do most to provide *me* with job security? However, in recent years, as we shall see, plenty of evidence has come to light suggesting that considerations of personal or family economic prosperity are, at best, no more important than questions of national economic policy, the relative merits of nationalisation and private ownership of industry, the role of trade unions in society, and so on. These are considerations of a basically ideological character, for which the A–E schema makes virtually no allowance.

Before the 1970s there was certainly a close relationship between occupational class and party allegiance. Data collected by the Gallup Poll demonstrated that at no election between 1945 and 1966 did non-manual support for the Conservative Party average less than 68 per cent, while manual-worker support for the Labour Party averaged no less than 61 per cent. The wealthier the non-manual sub-group under observation, the greater the degree of Conservative commitment; the poorer the manual sub-group, the greater the adherence to the Labour Party. Even allowing for statistical error, and the crudeness of the categories employed, we are none the less justified in arguing that approximately two-thirds of both groups voted for their 'natural' class party. But if we accept this broad, major conclusion, we are duty-bound also to accept

Table 1.3 Conservative and Labour voting by occupational class, 1970–1987

Percentage supporting the Conservative Party

	ABC1	C2DE
1970	64	33
1974 (F)	53	24
1974 (O)	51	24
1979	60	35
1983	55	35
1987	54	35

Percentage supporting the Labour Party

1970	25	58
1974 (F)	22	57
1974 (O)	25	57
1979	23	50
1983	17	42
1987	18	42

Derived from: A. Heath, R. Jowell & J. Curtice, *How Britain Votes* (Pergamon, 1985) [1970–1983]; R.M. Worcester in *The Times*, 13 June 1987 [1987 data only].

another: that about a third of both groups did not vote in a class-based manner.

It may well be the case, as the authors of one recent monograph have observed, that 'despite the alleged erosion of working class solidarity in the 1950s, class voting remained at least as high in 1966 as it had been in 1945'.[3] But so did the level of non-class voting. In 1959, on the occasion of Harold Macmillan's successful appeal to the electorate to maintain the Conservatives in office because most people 'have never had it so good', 30 per cent of manual workers voted Tory, and only 57 per cent Labour. At the time of the Labour victory of 1964, over a third of the professional (AB) groups did not support the Conservatives. In 1966 this proportion was as high as 4 out of 10.

These historical trends are important not merely in themselves — they clearly belie the sweeping assertion that class was, at one time, 'the basis of British party politics';[4] they form the indispensable back-cloth against which the decay of class-based partisanship in more recent years must be viewed. The broad pattern of this decline since 1970 is reproduced in Table 1.3.

The trends are so obvious—and so startling—as not, perhaps, to require much background comment. But, in studying these figures, it is important for us to recall that they relate to a 17-year period of British history that was replete with the rhetoric and reality of so-called 'class conflict'.

The Heath government enacted a tough Industrial Relations Act in 1971, aimed at curbing trade-union militancy. There were major industrial stoppages in 1972 and 1973, and the miners' strike in February 1974 precipitated the general election that brought Conservative rule to an end. During the period of Labour rule, 1974–9, unemployment rose to 1.6 million (August 1977), and the 'Winter of Discontent' (1978–9), while it did not of itself bring down the government, was a reflection of deeply felt anger on the part of the public-sector unions at government curbs on wage bargaining. Mrs Thatcher's first term of office saw unemployment pass the figure of 3 million (over 12 per cent of the workforce, the highest percentage since 1932); during her second term this figure was exceeded (it peaked at over 3.2 million in July 1986), there was a bitter and protracted miners' strike, and further legislation aimed at curbing the rights of trade unions was enacted, effectively re-establishing in some respects the situation that had existed before the Trade Disputes Act of 1906!

The electoral result of all this turmoil and antagonism was, however, that manual-worker support for the Conservative Party rose (even if it had simply remained static, this would have been cause enough for comment), non-manual support for both Conservative and Labour Parties fell, and—most remarkable of all—the proportion of manual workers, casual workers and state pensioners prepared to vote Labour also fell. In the 1980s, for the first time in post-1945 electoral history, a majority of the manual working classes no longer voted for what was, until very recently, thought of as their natural class party.

In trying to explain these developments (which, while amounting as they do to a political revolution, are in turn the outcome of a social revolution), political scientists have viewed with increasing scepticism the contemporary relevance, for their purposes, of the A–E classification regarded as standard in the 1950s and 1960s. The C2 class used to be thought of as embracing the archetypal working-class voter: one who had had a minimum of formal education; who was in a manual occupation and belonged to a trade union; who, typically, lived in accommodation rented from a local authority; and who, above all, felt him or herself to be working class. Categories A, B and C1 comprised those who had progressed to some form of further education, did not belong to a trade union, lived in housing they had bought or were buying

Table 1.4 Relationship between class characteristics and political preferences

	Con (%)	Lab (%)
Upper-middle class		
Four characteristics	78	15
One characteristic	40	47
Lower-middle class		
Four characteristics	69	22
One characteristic	35	57
Working class		
Four characteristics	19	73
One characteristic	59	30

Source: R. Rose (ed.), *Electoral Behavior* (Glencoe, Illinois, 1974).

themselves (or were renting from a private landlord), and who regarded themselves as middle class.

By the early 1970s these descriptions held true only of a small minority of the British voting public; less than 10 per cent of the electorate exhibited all the C2 characteristics, and only about 12 per cent conformed to the 'classic' middle-class pattern. As the extent of this non-conformity increased, so the degree of class-based realignment became more marked. The effect on party support is illustrated in Table 1.4.

At the four-characteristic level, class-voting was still, at the beginning of the 1970s, a reality; at the level of one characteristic it was not. Within the upper-middle-class sector (this would include professional, salaried voters), those with only one middle-class characteristic (say, their level of education) were more likely to vote Labour than Conservative, while more working-class voters with only one working-class characteristic voted Conservative than Labour.

At that time, over 45 per cent of the electorate possessed no more than two characteristics that matched their occupational status. Since then, the pace of social change has accelerated at such a rate as to have resulted in the creation of a virtually new electorate, to which the old categorical stereotypes can no longer safely be applied. These stereotypes made no provision for the self-employed, who are to be found at all levels of society, from the learned professions and the farmers to shopkeepers and skilled artisans working on their own account. Self-employed people may well belong to a relevant professional association, but they are less likely to identify themselves with the values and aspirations of traditional trade unionism. In particular, they will certainly be receptive to policies designed to favour private and individual enterprise.

By contrast, employed manual workers who are engaged at weekly, or perhaps hourly, wage-rates, under the constant supervision of managers, tend, as they have always done, to look to improvements in their level of remuneration and conditions of work through collective bargaining. The Labour Party was originally founded by and to serve the needs of these groups: it was (and constitutionally still is) the political arm of the trade-union movement. The contraction of both the movement and the size of the groups it serves are the inevitable consequence of the decline of the Victorian heavy and labour-intensive industries (coal, shipbuilding, iron and steel, transport), a decline that can be traced to the inter-war period but which has accelerated over the past quarter-century. Even in 1964 this traditional working class accounted for somewhat less than half the electorate (47 per cent); 20 years later the proportion had fallen to about a third.

The level of earnings of the self-employed depend on their own efforts; if they do not work they are not paid, but they are relatively free to choose their own hours of work and to set their own rates of pay, subject to market forces. Manual wage-labourers have no security of employment, little or no freedom to organise their working day, and relatively modest levels of sick-pay, pension entitlements and redundancy provisions; these may consist entirely of, or be little better than, state social-security benefits. Those who are paid salaries are in an altogether different position. Whatever the level of remuneration of salaried employees (the level is not likely to be low compared with wage-earners), their security of employment is relatively good, they will, in all probability, enjoy substantial fringe benefits and, unlike wage-labourers, they will have before them an incremental career structure.

The Victorians had difficulty accommodating the 'salariat' within the upper classes–bourgeoisie–labourer spectrum. Strictly speaking, and certainly from a legal point of view, those who drew a salary were members of the working classes. But the incongruity of bracketing bank managers with dock workers soon became apparent; so the salariat was classified as middle class. When the salariat was small in size, even this anomaly did not matter too much from a political point of view. Even in 1964, those who drew a salary accounted for, perhaps, 18 per cent of the electorate. It has been estimated that by the end of the 1980s no less than 27 per cent of all electors belong to the salaried classes.

Observers of British electoral politics have concentrated on the salariat because although in purely occupational terms it embraces a very wide variety of activities (from chairmen of companies through the managerial classes to very junior administrators), in *value* terms it is remarkably homogeneous. Thus, members of the salariat are not merely opposed to nationalisation; they have become much more entrenched in this opposition over the past 20 years. Housing provides another example. Since 1964 the proportion of the salariat who are owner-occupiers has risen from 13 per cent to roughly a quarter. For most people, home-ownership represents the largest single instance of wealth accumulation during their lifetime. Those who are buying their own homes want their property rights preserved; they pay attention to the state of the financial markets, which in turn influences the rate of interest they pay to the banks and building societies. As Heath, Jowell & Curtice have shown, owner-occupiers are demonstrably more likely than council-tenants to favour privatisation, and to be critical of government policies designed to redistribute wealth.[5]

The extension of home-ownership in Britain has had major political implications. In 1945 only a quarter of the national housing stock was in owner-occupation; over a half was located in the privately rented sector, and 12 per cent was rented from local authorities. Most families in Britain were thus tenants, not owner-occupiers, and they had a natural interest in policies designed to control and subsidise the rents they paid. Of course, this did not mean that every tenant was a Labour supporter; but it did give the edge to Labour housing policies, especially the building of more council houses and opposition to a 'free-for-all' in the level of rents landlords could legally charge.

The number of dwellings rented within the private sector fell steeply after the end of the Second World War, but the proportion rented from local authorities grew until, at the end of the 1970s, it stood at 32 per cent of the total. When Mrs Thatcher came to power in 1979, 55 per cent of the housing stock was owner-occupied. Although, therefore, it might be argued that the drift towards owner-occupation (an increase of just under one per cent *per annum* since 1945) had been to the advantage of the Conservatives, the expansion of the local-authority sector helped Labour—though not to quite the same extent.

The political behaviour of voters who live in different types of housing stock is set out in Table 1.5. The broad conclusion to which these figures seem to point is that the creation of a 'home-owning democracy' has not been of especial benefit to the Conservative Party. Indeed, viewed in the longer term, Conservative support among all voters who own their own homes was not much higher in 1987 than it had been in 1974 (the increase is about 3 per cent), while Labour support among local-authority tenants, although it increased by 6 per cent since 1983, only recovered in 1987 to the position recorded 13 years previously.

Table 1.5 Voting behaviour by housing tenure (%), 1983 and 1987

	Conservative		Labour		Alliance	
	1983	**1987**	**1983**	**1987**	**1983**	**1987**
Owner–occupiers						
All	52	50	19	23	28	25
Middle class	58	57	12	15	29	26
Working class	46	43	25	32	27	23
Council-tenants						
All	26	22	47	56	24	19
Middle class	32	28	39	41	25	24
Working class	25	21	49	58	24	18

Source: MORI data, *Sunday Times*, 14 June 1987.

In fact, the advantage that has accrued to the Conservative Party through long-term changes in the structure of the housing market is greater than might be suggested by this simple scenario. In 1980 the Conservative government legislated to permit the tenants of local authorities to buy the council houses in which they lived. In this way, by 1983 over half a million council houses and flats had been sold to the people living in them. By 1987 just over two-thirds of the electorate lived in their own homes; only 23 per cent were council tenants, and those who rented privately amounted to just 7 per cent. In 1987 the Labour Party proved much more popular among council-tenants (the Labour lead over the Conservatives amounted to 34 percentage points) than among owner-occupiers (the Conservative lead over Labour here amounted to 27 points). But it cannot be of much comfort to a political party to know that its popularity is increasing among a section of the voting public that has dwindled in size, and whose contraction will certainly continue.

Between 1964 and 1983 the proportion of the electorate represented by working-class home-owners only increased from 15 to 16 per cent; but between 1983 and 1987 it rose spectacularly, to 31 per cent. There are now almost as many working-class as middle-class owner-occupiers, and working-class home-owners outnumber working-class council-tenants. The phasing-out of municipal housing does not automatically increase the number of Conservative supporters; but it does eat into one of the traditional areas of Labour strength.

In 1987 Conservative support was more than twice a strong as

Labour support among all owner-occupiers, and even among working-class owner-occupiers the Conservative Party was still the most popular. As with occupational-class voting as a whole, a development of this sort suggests that we need to differentiate as much between different *types* of working-class voter as between different sectors of the middle classes.

The differentiation can be taken several stages further. In 1983 the proportion of all manual workers who lived in the South of England was roughly the same as that living in the North and in Scotland: 36 per cent and 38 per cent respectively. By 1987 the proportions were 40 per cent and 37 per cent. Table 1.6 shows how these voters divided at the two elections. In 1987 Labour managed to widen, to its advantage, the gap between its share of the working-class vote in the North and that taken by the Conservatives; but in the South the Conservative lead increased to 18 percentage points. In the North and Scotland, which are areas of declining population, over half the manual vote went to Labour; in the South Labour's performance among these voters was scarcely better than that of the Alliance.

The argument can be further developed, by breaking down the manual vote along two other fault-lines that have become ever more distinctive under (and, partly, as a result of) Thatcherite Conservatism. Since 1979 over a third of state-owned industries, employing more than 600,000 people, have been returned to private ownership. One in five of the adult population now owns shares, most of which have been acquired as a result of the privatisation schemes. First, therefore, we can ask whether employment in the public and private sectors produces significantly different voting outcomes. Table 1.7 gives the answer.

In 1983 the Labour lead over the Conservatives among public-sector manual workers was 17 points, and among private-sector workers there was just a 1-point difference; in 1987 Labour did not manage to widen these gaps. As the size of the private sector grows in relation to the public, the admittedly very large Labour lead in the public sector will become less important; in the expanding private sector the Labour and Conservative Parties will be much more evenly matched.

Secondly, we can ask whether membership of a trade union has any bearing on political loyalties. Table 1.8 gives the figures for every election since that of October 1974.

1983 was the peak year for Conservative support amongst members of trade unions, but the fall in support since then has been very modest. The Labour recovery in 1987 was achieved largely at the expense of the Alliance, not the Tories. Since 1979 Labour has been unable to retain even half the trade-union vote and, though it remains the largest single recipient of the trade-union franchise, we must add that as a proportion of the total

Table 1.6 The North–South divide among manual workers

	North/Scotland		South	
	1983	**1987**	**1983**	**1987**
Conservative	32	29	42	46
Labour	42	57	26	28
Alliance	26	15	32	26

Source: BBC/Gallup.

Table 1.7 The manual vote by occupational sector

	Public sector		Private sector	
	1983	**1987**	**1983**	**1987**
Conservative	29	32	36	38
Labour	46	49	37	39
Alliance	25	19	27	23

Source: BBC/Gallup.

Table 1.8 The trade-union vote, 1974–1987

	1974 (O)	**1979**	**1983**	**1987**
Conservative	23	31	32	30
Labour	55	53	39	48
Lib/Alliance	16	16	28	22

Source: Louis Harris (1974); BBC/Gallup (1979–1987).

electorate trade unionists are a declining force. In 1974, when trade-union membership reached a post-war record of 11.8 million (about 30 per cent of the electorate), Labour polled only 55 per cent of the votes trade unionists cast. In 1987 Labour polled 48 per cent of the votes of a trade-union movement that had shrunk to only 23 per cent of the electorate. As with council-tenants, therefore, Labour clings to the largest share of an asset that is diminishing both in value and extent.

Considerations such as these have led some observers to conclude that it is misleading even to speak of one 'manual working class' in relation to the political sociology of contemporary Britain. Professor Ivor Crewe, of Essex University, refers instead to a 'traditional working class of the council estates, the public sector, industrial Scotland and the North, and the old industrial unions', and a 'new working class . . . of the South'.[6] That a division of this type exists also among middle-class voters can be similarly demonstrated. Thus, while around 59 per cent of the professional and managerial electorate voted Conservative in 1987, only a third of university graduates did so; Labour polled 14 per cent of the professional and managerial classes but over twice this proportion among the graduates. The largest single slice of the graduate vote went to the Alliance in 1987, though it had gone to the Conservatives in 1983.

But university graduates form only a very small proportion of the electorate. The expansion of the salariat, coupled with the contraction of the public sector, has had a much bigger impact. In 1987 the Conservative Party attracted the votes of less than half the public-sector salariat, but almost two-thirds of private-sector salaried employees; in the public sector the Conservative proportion fell by 4 per cent compared with 1983, but in the private sector it rose by 1 per cent. The Alliance was the beneficiary in the former case, and the loser in the latter; Labour made no headway at all in either category.

An examination of the present relationship between class and voting in Britain does not support the view that *no* relationship now exists, or that Britain has become a 'classless' society. The occupational class to which a voter belongs is still the single best predictor of his or her voting behaviour. But we must now be much more precise and particular about the categories we employ. It is dangerous, and blatantly complacent, for politicians to address themselves any longer to middle- and working-class voters in monolithic terms. In trying to understand the determinants of voting, the class framework that we use must therefore be more complex than that commonly employed 25 years ago. The British electorate has experienced class *re*alignment, not *de*alignment. Class has not withered away, but new occupational cleavages in society have promoted a new set of class–party relationships.

In the 1960s and early 1970s the major element in this process seems to have been the rise in the frequency of middle-class voters supporting Labour candidates; in 1964 17 per cent of Labour's total support was derived from non-manual workers, but by October 1974 this figure had grown to 27 per cent.[7] In the late 1970s and 1980s the rate of decline in non-manual support for the Conservatives became less steep (partly as a result of renewed middle-class support in the private sector), but Labour suffered a relatively more severe haemorrhage in its once very reliable support amongst manual workers.

The net result of these developments is that the political loyalties of different occupational classes have become more evenly spread between the Labour and Conservative Parties. The Labour Party has suffered most from these realignments, but it has suffered in another way too, which relates to a parallel process, whereby basic party loyalty has become more detached from attitudes towards particular areas of policy. To this process the term *de*alignment can accurately be applied.

The roots of partisan dealignment are to be found in changes in the constituent elements of political socialisation—the process whereby voters acquire their political attitudes and knowledge of political issues. In the 1950s and 1960s conventional wisdom, supported by empirical research, taught that the major elements in political socialisation were provided by the family into which a voter was born, the home in which the voter grew up and the locality in which the voter lived. These elements are still important, but not so important as was once the case. Locality—the neighbourhood in which people live—may still play a part. A working-class trade unionist whose Labour attachment is weak or weakening may perhaps receive some encouragement and support in his Labour commitment simply from the fact of living in a staunchly Labour constituency, working alongside rock-solid Labour workmates, meeting them in pubs and clubs. The temptation to vote Conservative, or Alliance, will diminish. But if such a voter lives in a Conservative environment, the temptation may prove too great.

This line of argument may explain why, in 1987, only a quarter of trade unionists voted Conservative in the North of England, but over a third in the South, and it may also help to explain the increasingly regional location of party support. But, even if the argument has some merit, it is unlikely to constitute more than a partial explanation. Another element in the equation is that those constituencies which are safest from Labour's point of view probably have weak Conservative constituency associations (and vice-versa), which run campaigns more or less out of habit.

In any case, regional differences in political support are not so much explanations of voting behaviour as reflections of it. Regional differences, that is, are in the main outcomes of the make-up of regional electorates. We know that since the 1960s the influence of the family and the home have become much less pervasive than was formerly the case. The mass media—especially television, which reached 95 per cent of homes in 1970 (the 1970 general election was the first in which the voting age was reduced to 18)— provide alternative standards, and there are more opportunities for travel.

Partisanship hardens with age: the older a voter becomes, the more unlikely he or she is to switch to another party. But if the degree of partisan commitment is weak to begin with, the hardening process is likely to take much longer and, over a number of generations, may result in the formation of an electorate that is much less partisan (in the sense of the Conservative–Labour dichotomy) overall. Growth in support for 'third' parties is one indication that this is taking place, and we have already noted (see Tables 1.1 and 1.2) that the Alliance and the nationalist parties have benefited as a result.

Another way of measuring this trend is to ask voters how strongly—if at all—they feel about their commitment to either of the two major parties. The British Election Study at the University of Essex found that between 1964 and October 1974 there was a marked diminution of partisan commitment among successive age-groups. During this period the partisan strength of the youngest group of voters (aged between 20 and 27 in 1964), measured on a scale ranging from 0 for non-identifiers to 3 for very strong identifiers, declined from 1.97 to 1.82; for those who were aged between 28 and 35 in 1964 the decline was from 1.98 to 1.88. These groups alone (and it is noteworthy that the Essex study found weakening partisan commitment among all age-groups), now, in the late 1980s, comprise about half the total electorate.

Between 1970 and 1979 partisan commitment weakened still further, as we might expect. The proportion of the electorate prepared to identify with either the Labour or the Conservative Party remained high (over 75 per cent), but the number of strong identifiers shrank from 39 per cent to just 20 per cent over the course of this decade.[8] Although, therefore, the bulk of the votes cast (as in 1983 and 1987) are cast in favour of the two major parties, only about a fifth of this support can be reckoned as coming from a core of dedicated partisans. The obverse of this is that Labour and Conservative propagandists must work much harder to marshal their voters to the polls. Yet this task has become more difficult for Labour than for the Conservatives. Labour is a party that has always contrived to project a class image, and to appeal for support on a class basis. Its existence is justified partly on the grounds that 'working-class' people allegedly suffer deprivation and discrimination simply because of their class, which makes life much harder for them than for the middle classes.

Table 1.9 Flow of the vote, 1979–1983 (A) and 1983–1987 (B)

	Con		Lab		SDP/Lib		Non-voters		Under 18	
	A	**B**	**A**	**B**	**A**	**B**	**A**	**B**	**A**	**B**
Con	77	77	7	4	14	10	22	21	28	28
Lab	4	5	63	75	9	12	12	19	17	24
SDP/Lib	13	12	22	11	72	70	14	14	20	14
Other	—	—	1	1	—	1	—	1	2	1
Non-voters	6	6	7	8	5	8	52	45	32	32

Source: BBC/Gallup.

What is the reality nowadays? In their investigation of voting behaviour in the 1960s, David Butler and Donald Stokes found that only a quarter of their respondents thought of themselves as being to the 'left' or 'right' in politics. Over two-thirds did not think of themselves in terms of 'left' or 'right' at all. Even among those electors who believed in a relationship between class and party, only a minority saw the relationship in terms of class *conflict*.[9] By 1979 the proportion of manual workers prepared to declare themselves, spontaneously, as 'working class' had fallen from 46 per cent (1964) to 39 per cent, whereas those who thought of themselves as 'middle class' actually rose from 6 to 8 per cent.[10] By the early 1980s most voters, whether they labelled themselves working or middle class, no longer believed that their class status made any difference to their lives.[11]

The disproportionate effect that these changes in attitude have had on party support may be estimated by examining the 'flow' of the vote at the two most recent general elections; the data is set out in Table 1.9.

Seventy-seven per cent of those who had voted Conservative in 1979 remained loyal in 1983; the same result obtained in 1987 with respect to 1983 Conservative support. Loyal Labour voters were less in evidence on both occasions (63 per cent and 75 per cent respectively). Labour has been less successful in attracting former Liberal and Alliance voters, and significantly less successful than the Conservatives among the youngest members of the electorate: in 1983 28 per cent of those too young to have voted in 1979 supported Conservative candidates, whereas only 17 per cent became Labour supporters; there was some improvement in Labour's performance among such voters in 1987, but the proportion still did not match the figure achieved on the Conservative side.

To demonstrate partisan dealignment is relatively easy; to explain it is fraught with difficulties. We have already seen that the class–party relationship supposed to have existed in mid-century was—in the strictest sense—a myth. The phenomenon of working-class Conservatism used to be explained in terms of deference, and there was, no doubt, a great deal of truth in this. But we would be seriously misleading ourselves if we refused to allow that in the past the Conservative Party attracted working-class votes on purely pragmatic and programmatic grounds: jingoism, 'khaki' elections, protective tariffs, anti-immigration policies, embryonic welfare and generous housing policies have all proved vote winners with Conservatively-inclined working men and women.

Nor should we lull ourselves into uncritical acceptance of another once-popular theory—that of *embourgeoisement*—according to which working-class solidarity with Labour politics has been undermined by post-war affluence and the acquisition, by manual workers, of a range of consumer durables and package holidays on the Mediterranean coast. The popularity of this thesis during the 1950s is easily understood, because it offered a neat explanation for a string of Labour defeats at a time of growing national prosperity and full employment. But it cannot be transported into the 1980s, when an equal number of Labour defeats have taken place at a time of economic stagnation and uncertainty, and of the return of mass unemployment. The irrelevance of *embourgeoisement* to contemporary British politics is demonstrated in Table 1.10, which tabulates the political preferences of unemployed voters.

In 1983 Labour could not rely on the votes of even half those electors who were without employment at the time of the poll; in 1987 almost a third of the unemployed votes still went to Conservative candidates.

A more plausible—but certainly not a total—explanation for partisan dealignment is provided by what is seen as the rise (or, more accurately, the return) of issue-voting. This means, quite simply, that a more discerning breed of voter has entered the political stage, better informed (perhaps because of more sophisticated media coverage) and willing to vote for candidates on the basis of policies, rather than for parties on the basis of images. If we live in a more consumer-orientated society, then, by this argument, a growing number of voters decide how to vote according to which set of policies on offer represents the 'best buy' for them at a particular time. 'Brand loyalty' may still count for something, but cannot be taken for granted; what a voter decides is the 'best buy' at one election may no longer constitute the 'best buy' next time around.

In the context of recent election campaigns, two aspects of issue-

Table 1.10 The unemployed vote, 1979–1987

	1979	1983	1987
Con	40	30	32
Lab	49	44	51
SDP/Lib	11	26	17

Source: BBC/Gallup.

voting need to be addressed here. First, what issues, *in the opinion of voters*, are most important? Secondly, how does the answer to this question correlate with the answer to another, namely what issues do the major political parties consider most important? At the elections of 1979, 1983 and 1987 the BBC/Gallup Survey asked voters to name the two most important issues influencing their choice on polling day. The five topics cited most frequently in 1987 were (in descending order of popularity) unemployment, defence, the National Health Service, education and pensions. All five appeared in answers to similar questions posed in 1979 and 1983; concern with prices, which had figured in these elections, was absent in 1987.

Taken at face value, these issues might be thought of as ones upon which, on the whole, Labour was bound to win support. In 1987 most voters thought that unemployment had worsened, that the problem of ever-lengthening waiting lists at state-run hospitals had become more acute, and that the standard of education at state schools had fallen. But all the available evidence points to the fact that many voters did not *blame* the Conservative government for these shortcomings, and that those who did tended to defect to the Alliance as much as to Labour. We have already noted the strength of Conservative popularity even amongst voters who were actually experiencing the dole queue. Pensioners, who make up about 23 per cent of the electorate, defected from the Conservatives only to the extent of 2 to 3 per cent. Defence was clearly a vote-loser for the Labour Party, for reasons which will be explained in Chapter Two. On this issue, as on the others, more electors thought that more viable and effective, lasting solutions would come from a Conservative government than from a government of any other political complexion. In any case, whatever criticisms the unemployed and the pensioners might have levelled at Mrs Thatcher's administration, almost half the electorate felt that the nation's economic prospects had improved under her leadership; more importantly, only 28 per cent considered that between 1983 and 1987 their own personal financial circumstances had deteriorated.

When prompted by the pollsters to rank particular problems, voters no doubt give honest answers; but we must beware of concluding that these particular issues form the sole basis of electoral choice. In 1983 the single most important consideration bearing upon individual decision-making in the polling booth was the general state of the economy. It was this, rather than any so-called 'Falklands Factor', that contributed most to the Conservative recovery, which began some months before the outbreak of war in the South Atlantic.[12] The levelling off in the unemployment figures, falling exchange rates that increased the competitiveness of British industry (so leading to higher pay and more opportunities for overtime earnings), and the tax-cutting budget of March 1982 all conspired to increase voters' trust in the Conservative Party. The defeat of General Galtieri's invasion force merely bolstered a sense of confidence which was already moving back in Mrs Thatcher's direction.

So it was in 1987. A clear majority of voters felt that the unemployment situation would not improve under the Conservatives, that racial harmony was more likely to deteriorate, that the standard of provision in the welfare services would stagnate.[13] Yet, on the key issues of low inflation and low income tax, more than two-thirds believed that the country was safer in Conservative hands. In picking out, for special treatment in its manifesto, topics such as an 'anti-poverty programme', a freer National Health Service, women's rights, equal treatment for ethnic minorities, and even crime prevention (significantly, the subject of law-and-order did not figure at all in the rankings voters gave of the most important criteria influencing their voting intentions), the Labour Party chose to address the electorate on matters which were either of marginal interest to them, or of no interest at all; Labour fought the election on a make-believe battleground. For, whatever voters felt on individual items of policy, their collective view was that Britain had become more prosperous under Conservative rule, and that the best way to guarantee such prosperity in the future was to guarantee Mrs Thatcher another term of office.

The situation thus described—of an electorate that is driven largely by selfish motives—may well appear grim and morally uncomfortable. It is none the less founded upon empirical evidence and it is also grounded in realism. Democracy consists in providing a government that gives voters what they want, rather than what politicians think they ought to have. By pursuing frankly populist policies the Conservative Party has, under Mrs Thatcher's leadership, ingratiated itself with sufficient sections of an increasingly fragmented and sectionalised electorate to secure the lion's share of the votes, even if these amount neither to a

Table 1.11 Regional share of the vote (%), 1987

	Con		Lab		Alliance		SNP/P. Cymru	
Scotland	24	(−4)	42	(+7)	22	(−5)	13	(+1)
Wales	30	(−1)	45	(+7)	18	(−5)	7	(−1)
N. England	37	(−2)	42	(+5)	21	(−3)		
Midlands/Southern England	51	(+1.5)	24	(+1.5)	24	(−3)		

majority of the voters nor to a majority of the electors. But this support is not evenly spread across the whole of Great Britain (while in Northern Ireland, of course, wholly different circumstances apply). It remains now to give some consideration to regional patterns and national variations in political support in England, Scotland and Wales.

Table 1.11 provides a comparative view of the share of the vote obtained by the major parties in Scotland, Wales and two geographical sub-divisions of England in the 1987 election; the figures in brackets show the rise or fall in this share compared with 1983. Given that the Ulster Unionist alliance with the Conservative Party collapsed in the early 1970s, in only one of the four countries that make up the United Kingdom can the Conservatives claim to have 'won' in 1987. In Scotland the Conservatives obtained some 88,000 votes less than in 1983, and saw their parliamentary representation fall from 21 MPs to just ten; Labour picked up an extra nine seats, and the Alliance and the Scottish National Party one each. In Wales the Alliance and Plaid Cymru also increased their parliamentary representation by one seat each, Labour gained four and the Conservatives lost six. In the North of England the net result of modest falls in the Conservative and Alliance shares of the poll was to give Labour an extra six seats compared with the previous Parliament.

The apparent renaissance of Scottish and Welsh nationalism needs to be placed in perspective. Support for Plaid Cymru is grounded in cultural and linguistic rather than in political separatism. Founded in 1925, the party made no electoral impact until the dramatic victory of its President, Gwynfor Evans, at the Carmarthen by-election of July 1966; by October 1974 its parliamentary representation had increased to four MPs, and its share of the Welsh vote to 10.8 per cent. But these victories, and the leverage which its successful candidates were able to exert over the minority Labour government in the late 1970s, masked more fundamental weaknesses.

The strength of Plaid Cymru was rooted in a backlash by rural, Welsh-speaking areas against government (some would say, mis-government) from London, and also in a revolt against complacent (and in some cases corrupt) local Labour Parties whose total domination of Welsh politics had gone practically unchallenged and unchecked for the better part of half a century. Plaid Cymru's penetration of urban areas has been spasmodic and transitory. Since 1979 its share of the Welsh vote has declined without respite (8.1 per cent in 1979, 7.8 per cent in 1983 and 7.3 per cent in 1987) but, more significantly, this support has contracted into the Welsh-speaking areas of north and west Wales. In 1987 Plaid Cymru managed to save only six deposits (Caernarfon, Meirionnydd Nant Conwy and Ynys Mon, which it won, plus Carmarthen, Ceredigion & Pembroke North and Llanelli) and came bottom of the poll in 29 of the 38 Welsh seats.

The increase in Plaid Cymru's parliamentary representation was, therefore, more of a technical than a genuine success; the capture of Ynys Mon (Anglesey) from the Conservatives followed the well-publicised withdrawal of the Conservative MP, Keith Best, who was subsequently convicted of making multiple British Telecom share applications. The election of 1987 marked the end of a period of Conservative advance in Wales, but it must also be said that the Labour recovery was a qualified one: in the 1950s and 1960s Labour never failed to poll less than 56 per cent of the Welsh vote (in 1951 and 1966 the proportion was over 60 per cent). Labour's performance in Wales in 1987 amounted to the party's second worst result there since 1945.

In Scotland the 1987 result marked the continuation of a trend observable since 1955, the last occasion upon which the Conservative Party attracted the support of over half the Scottish voters. Labour has so far failed to regain the levels of support that came its way in Scotland in the 1950s and 1960s (in 1966 Labour polled almost 50 per cent of the Scottish vote), but given the history of Scottish politics since 1983 it would have been surprising indeed had Labour not been able to improve upon its more recent general election performances there. Scottish voters have been able to compile a formidable list of complaints stemming from the Conservative government's handling of Scottish issues, and these complaints, all well-founded, have attracted support from within the Scottish Conservative Party. A revaluation of properties led to heavy increases in Scottish domestic rates, which were replaced by a community charge, or poll tax; the closure of the Gartcosh steel plant had left a question mark over the future of the entire Scottish iron and steel industry. More generally, the decline of heavy industry has been more severe in Scotland than elsewhere; the boom created by the demands of the North Sea oil industry in its explorative phase is now over. At the time of the general election unemployment in Scotland was higher than in any other part of the United Kingdom except Northern Ireland and the North of England.

Support for the creation of some form of local assembly in Edinburgh, to which powers would be devolved from Westminster, is high even among Scottish voters who identify with the Conservative Party.[14] Yet the Scottish National Party (formed 1928) has been unable to capitalise upon this situation. Support for Scottish nationalism has been more evenly spread between rural and urban areas than support for nationalism in Wales; the SNP is a truly nationalist party, believing in Scottish independence, not just devolved government. However, most Scots (about two-thirds according to a MORI poll in April 1988) do not wish to see their country moving in this direction. In October 1974, with no less than eleven MPs, the Scottish National Party, though still the third Scottish party in terms of seats, was the second (after Labour) in terms of votes cast. Since then, however, in parliamentary terms, it has been a party in retreat, and although there was a very modest rise in its support in 1987 compared with 1983, the gain of one seat was offset by the defeat of the party leader, Gordon Wilson, at Dundee East.[15]

There are two ways of approaching the results of the 1987 election in Scotland and Wales. We can regard them as special cases, the product of unique political systems. In Scotland and Wales, unlike England, the contest was a genuine four-horse race, even if two of the horses were palpably weaker than the front-runners. Especially in Scotland, factors (such as the shadow of the community charge) were in operation which were clearly of little consequence in the rest of the United Kingdom. All this is true. But there are also strong grounds for viewing what happened in Wales and Scotland as merely particular examples of a strong regional and social bias (for example, over support for Labour among council-tenants) that was to be observed throughout England.

After the 1983 general election it was said that 'two nations' had emerged: a relatively prosperous South, largely Tory in allegiance, and a relatively poor North, where Labour was still strong. This picture, though obviously oversimplified, had a basic truth about it, if we agree to regard the 'two nations' as socially as well as geographically based. In general, wherever unemployment was high (say, over 12 per cent of the workforce) the swing to the Conservatives was low (usually under 4 per cent); in some cases (for example, the most urban Scottish and North-of-England seats) there was a strong swing to Labour. But in most areas of low unemployment (under 7 per cent) the swing to the Conservatives was in excess of 6 per cent. In Greater London the Tories did measurably better in the outer boroughs (where unemployment was below 5.7 per cent) than in the inner city.

This socio-political cleavage was widened and deepened in 1987. In London, the South-East and the South-West Labour managed to increase its share of the vote by less than 2 per cent; but in the Midlands the increase was above 2 per cent, in the North-West, Yorkshire and Humberside it was above 5 per cent, and in the North-East above 6 per cent. Throughout Britain, in those constituencies where unemployment was above average, Labour's share of the vote increased by 6 per cent, while the Conservative share fell by over 2 per cent.

The relatively poor performance of the Conservative Party in the North of England, Wales and Scotland in 1987 certainly gives further ammunition to those who believe that mainland Britain is now divided into two nations. The Conservatives emerged from that election holding less than a third of the Scottish, Welsh and Northern English seats, but over three-quarters of those located in the Midlands and the South. Yet the Labour Party cannot derive much comfort from this situation. In 1987 Labour did best in those areas where it was already strong. At Islwyn, in the heart of the South Wales coalfield, Labour's share of the vote leapt from 59.3 to 71.3 per cent; but (of course) only one Labour MP, Neil Kinnock, was returned there. The Westminster Parliament is not elected on the basis of any system whereby a party is necessarily and proportionately rewarded, in terms of seats, if there is an increase in its popular support.

Moreover, in the main Labour did well only in areas of static or declining population. The major areas of population increase in the 1980s have been East Anglia, South-East England (excluding Greater London) and the South-West; these are also the most prosperous areas of the country, measured in terms of average weekly income of households (about £50 higher in the South-East than in the North) and levels of unemployment. Even in Greater London, which the Labour Party once dominated, over half the seats are now held by the Conservatives; outside Greater London, in the South-East, Labour holds just one seat to the Conservatives' 107. In southern England and East Anglia as a whole (roughly the area south of a line drawn from the Severn Estuary to the Wash) the Alliance won six seats, Labour 26, but the Conservatives no less than 228.

It is this which, in large measure, explains the mechanics of Mrs Thatcher's 1987 triumph, and why she and her party have every reason to feel confident about their electoral prospects in the foreseeable future.

NOTES

1. In 1945, in exceptional circumstances, Labour achieved a swing of 11.8 per cent; the largest conventional swing since then has been 5.2 per cent (to the Conservatives) in 1979.
2. The 15 by-elections that took place in Northern Ireland on 23 January 1986 are excluded from this calculation.
3. A. Heath, R. Jowell & J. Curtice (1985), *How Britain Votes*, Oxford, Pergamon Press, p.29.
4. P.G.J. Pulzer (3rd edn, 1975), *Political Representation and Elections in Britain*, London, Allen & Unwin, p. 102.
5. Heath, Jowell & Curtice, p. 48.
6. *The Guardian*, 15 June 1987.
7. I. Crewe, B. Sarlvik & J. Alt, 'Partisan Dealignment in Britain, 1964–1974', *British Journal of Political Science*, vol. vii (1977).
8. P. Dunleavy, 'Voting and the Electorate', in H. Drucker, P. Dunleavy, A. Gamble & G. Peele (eds., 1984 edn), *Developments in British Politics*, London, Macmillan, p.41.
9. D. Butler & D. Stokes (2nd edn, 1974), *Political Change in Britain*, London, Macmillan, pp. 85, 468.
10. D. Robertson (1984), *Class and the British Electorate*, Oxford, Basil Blackwell, p. 87.
11. Robertson, p.95.
12. D. Saunders, H. Ward & D. Marsh, 'Government Popularity and the Falklands War: A Reassessment', *British Journal of Political Science*, vol. xvii (1987).
13. *Sunday Times*, 14 June 1987.
14. M. Dyer in the *Glasgow Herald*, 30 June 1987.
15. The Govan by-election (10 November 1988) resulted in a most convincing SNP victory over Labour, but its long-term implications need to be treated with caution, since the seat has once before been captured by the SNP (November 1973), but reverted to Labour at the February 1974 general election. At Pontypridd (23 February 1989) Plaid Cymru increased its share of the vote from 5.3 to 25.3 per cent; but this still fell very far short of posing a serious threat to Labour's retention of the seat.

2. Labour: Two Parties in One

Historians who write about the development of party politics in Britain in the second half of the twentieth century are bound to devote a great deal of space to explaining the rapid rise and equally rapid decline of Labour as a credible party of government. Even if the fortunes of Labour revive in the 1990s, the party will have changed out of all recognition compared to that which Clement Attlee led to victory in 1945, and even to that which chose Harold Wilson as its leader in 1963. In the previous chapter we saw how economic and social developments have eroded Labour's electoral base. Here we shall concentrate on trying to understand why the Labour Party has failed to adapt itself to the new electoral map of Britain.

All political parties are coalitions, in the sense that groups with different but compatible interests will have come together to form an organisation—the party—capable of winning power, and so enabling each interest to have its demand satisfied. The process of forming and the rigours of maintaining the coalition will doubtless impose compromise. But such accommodations are unlikely to affect the party's overall structure; if they do, of course, the coalition may well fall apart. Over the past 150 years this has happened to the Conservative Party only once, in 1846, when Sir Robert Peel's determination to abolish the Corn Laws (which symbolised the protective attitude of the party towards its farming clientele) led to an irreversible split that kept the party out of office for most of the succeeding 20 years. When Disraeli led it to power once more, he made it clear that the clock could not be turned back; protection was kept off the Conservative agenda for the next half-century.

The Labour Party, by contrast, has never been able to put its past behind it. Ironically, its traditions exert a much stronger pull than do Conservative traditions over Conservative policies. Conservative politicians have on the whole displayed a robust courage in their ability to discard ideologies which are judged to be out of date; Labour has clung to its ideological roots as an adolescent does to a favourite childhood toy, to give a feeling of security and well-being as times become ever more complicated and turbulent. Moreover, it is questionable whether the elements in the Labour coalition are in fact fundamentally compatible. At times the horses hitched to the Labour wagon have pulled so strongly in different directions that the wagon itself has come to a sudden halt, spilling out some of its passengers and needing structural repairs.

The Labour Party was established in 1900, under the title of the Labour Representation Committee, as the political arm of the trade-union movement. There were already in existence in Britain two socialist parties, the Social-Democratic Federation (SDF) founded in 1883 by a Cambridge-educated stockbroker turned Marxist, Henry Hyndman, and the Independent Labour Party (ILP), formed by the socialist secretary of the Scottish Miners' Federation, James Keir Hardie. Neither the SDF nor the ILP ever became mass parties, largely because they were unable to convert the bulk of the trade unions to their vision of a socialist future. In sharp contrast to trade unions on the Continent (especially France and Germany), British trade unions were and have remained essentially pragmatic and inward looking, concerned above all with the welfare of their own members.

There had been manual working-class MPs elected since 1874, all under the umbrella of the Gladstonian Liberal Party. Within the trade-union movement 'Lib–Labism' was the prevailing political ethos. Socialism had appeared to make some headway in a limited number of unions in the early 1890s (the period of the so-called 'New Unionism'), but by the middle of the decade the Lib–Labers had been able to fight off this challenge; in 1895 the TUC agreed to rule changes (including the institution of the 'block' vote) designed to curb socialist influence. The decision of the 1899 TUC to establish what became the Labour Representation Committee and, in 1906, the Labour Party, was due, quite simply, to a desire to reverse, by political means, a disturbing anti-union trend in legal judgements at this time. It is true that many trade unions were also exercised by the evident unwillingness of local Liberal Associations to adopt more working men as candidates. But the LRC specifically rejected a call from the SDF to adopt a socialist programme.

Instead, the LRC was formed as a federal body, on which trade unions together with the Fabian Society (a radical middle-class 'think-tank'), SDF, ILP and co-operative societies were represented, to establish 'a distinct Labour group [not party] in Parliament . . . [to promote] . . . legislation in the direct interests of labour'.

Labourism, not socialism, remained the prevailing ethos of the party, which itself remained a federation of affiliated organisations until the constitutional reforms of 1918 allowed for mass membership through a network of local constituency parties. Socialism was rejected for a number of reasons. The atheism of many of its proponents repelled those trade unionists who were committed Christians. The idea that the unions might create for themselves an independent political role, as Continental trade unions were doing, seemed to be a recipe for protracted internal strife. The egalitarianism upon which socialists placed so much emphasis was not generally supported. The British trade-union movement as it developed in the Victorian period was permeated with notions of hierarchy that have remained deeply ingrained: wage differentials were highly regarded, as they have continued to be. Above all, socialism preached state intervention and, therefore, a strengthening of the organs of central government. Many trade unionists regarded such a prospect as highly damaging to working-class interests, because the power of the state was a double-edged weapon: it could be used to better the lot of the poor, but it could also be used to restrict union activity.

Socialism remained a dirty word among many trade unionists well into the present century. It is a sobering thought that as late as 1921 a leading union organiser, Labour MP and future Labour Cabinet Minister, Jimmy Thomas (General Secretary of the National Union of Railwaymen), could deny on oath (in the course of a libel action against a Communist newspaper) that he harboured socialist persuasions. In 1918 the Labour Party had indeed adopted, as part of its new constitution, a commitment to work for 'the common ownership of the means of production'—not, it should be noted, 'distribution and exchange', which were added much later. But it soon became clear that this apparent commitment to socialism implied little more than the public ownership of activities which had already come under state control during the First World War. Capitalism was not to be overthrown, and there was certainly to be no shift to 'workers' control'—a phrase which now had unpleasant Bolshevik overtones. Rather, the economic system was to be made to function more efficiently in the interests of the nation as a whole.

Why and to what extent did out-and-out socialists acquiesce in this state of affairs? Some realised early on that a political party built upon trade-union foundations could not, in the British context, be transformed into a truly socialist organism (less still a revolutionary force), dedicated to the single-minded pursuit of an egalitarian, state-run society in which capitalism would be out-lawed, or at least heavily penalised, and in which all private property would be held at the mercy of central government. In 1903 the SDF severed its links with the LRC, whose reformist and exclusively parliamentary stance SDF members could no longer stomach. Ten years later the SDF and some other left-wing elements formed the British Socialist Party, which in 1920 sank its identity within the new Communist Party of Great Britain. Discussions between the Communist and Labour Parties on the possibility of the affiliation of the former to the latter foundered, as they were bound to do, because of the refusal of the Communist Party to renounce the revolutionary, non-parliamentary road to a socialist state.

But not all socialists broke with Labour politics. After 1918 Labour was determined to be, and to be seen to be, a non-revolutionary advocate of change within the parliamentary system. Some socialists (such as the famous 'Clydeside' group of Labour MPs that included John Wheatley and Manny Shinwell) accepted this framework because (especially with the imminent demise of the old Liberal Party) they saw in Labour the only hope for radical change in Britain. Other socialists ('crypto-communists'), such as Konni Zilliacus, elected in 1945 but later expelled (and still later re-elected), remained in the party not as secret agents of Joseph Stalin but because they continued to nurture the hope that the militant espousers of class warfare who held sway in their particular constituency parties would be able to win converts as unemployment worsened and poverty spread.

This did not happen, and socialists were never able to command majority support in the party; partly as a result, Labour played no part in the General Strike (1926), which was terminated when TUC leaders (notably Jimmy Thomas and Ernie Bevin) took fright at the prospect of its success, leaving the miners (on whose behalf the strike had been declared) to the mercy of the coalowners. In the aftermath of the collapse of the second Labour government (1931) there appears to have been a reaction in the socialist direction. Activists seized the opportunity provided by Ramsay MacDonald's betrayal of the party, and his agreement (endorsed by Thomas and a few others) to head a largely Conservative 'National' Govern-ment, to persuade the party to adopt policies far more radical than anything Labour had espoused hitherto. At the party Conferences of 1932, 1933 and 1934 'the establishment of socialism' was declared to be 'the main objective' of the Labour Party, which committed itself to the nationalisation of land, transport, electricity generation and distribution, water supply, coal, iron and steel and the joint-stock banks, as well as 'the common ownership of the means of production and distribution'. Moreover, the 1933 conference pledged itself in favour of the direct representation of trade unions on the boards of management of nationalised undertakings. 'Workers' control', Attlee declared in 1935, 'is . . . an essential part of the new order.'

The Conference debates of the early 1930s marked the high water mark of radical (as opposed to revolutionary) socialism as a significant policy-making force within the pre-war Labour Party; the 1934 programme (*For Socialism and Peace*) formed, in its essentials, the basis of the policy initiatives undertaken by the Labour government that came to power in July 1945. But no one could seriously argue that what Labour achieved between 1945 and 1951 amounted to 'socialism'. True, the basic utility industries were put under state ownership: the major airlines, the railways and canals, the road haulage industry, the coal mines, the gas and electricity industries, iron and steel, the Bank of England. Most of these measures were made necessary by post-war conditions; a Conservative government would have been hard pressed to have allowed the railways or the mines (both suffering from gross under-investment and lack of modernisation) to have remained in private hands.

We must also remind ourselves here that there is nothing particularly 'socialist' about public ownership *per se*. In 1844 Peel's Conservative government had legislated to allow the partial nationalisation of the railway industry; the aim was to ensure that the railways served the national interest, not to bring about a socialist society. In their nationalisation policies Attlee and Herbert Morrison (the architect of the public-corporation model for running industries taken into public ownership) conveniently forgot the Conference resolutions of the early 1930s and made no concessions to 'workers' control'. Trade unions were denied managerial status; public ownership was not going to be used as a means of shifting power within industrial concerns.

All in all, the post-war Attlee government took under public control only about 20 per cent of the national economy, encompassing some of the most under-capitalised and worn-out sectors of industry. The remaining 80 per cent were left in private hands. When Harold Wilson became head of the Board of Trade, in 1948, the government embarked on a policy of doing away with controls over this private sector, too. The basis of the government's economic policy was not state direction of private enterprise, but state assistance to help the recovery of capitalism. Morrison himself had declared bluntly that the nationalised undertakings were 'not ends in themselves', but that the object was 'to make possible organisation of a more efficient industry, rendering more public service'. And to the extent that society had become more efficient by 1951 (rather than, say, less class-ridden and less unequal), Attlee and his colleagues could congratulate themselves on having advanced the cause of socialism as they saw it!

In 1962 Hugh Dalton, a prominent member of Attlee's team and Chancellor of the Exchequer from 1945 to 1947, admitted in his memoirs that socialism had not actually been tried. 'We weren't really beginning our socialist programme until we had gone past all the public utilities . . . [he wrote] . . . which were publicly owned in nearly every capitalist country in the world.' How had it come about that the socialist promises of the early 1930s had not been fulfilled when the government had been swept into office with a massive majority of 146 seats and over 50 per cent of the votes cast in every constituency it had contested? To understand this, and to comprehend also how it was that leaders with eminent radical credentials such as Attlee (who had applauded George Lansbury for breaking the law in 1921 in order to secure better poor-law payments to the poor of Poplar) and Wilson (who resigned in 1950 over the imposition of modest health charges) have managed to break effortlessly with their militant past, we need to examine the part played in the development of the Labour Party by what has come to be known as 'Social Democracy'.

In its early years Labour was little more than a pressure group, operating within an electoral system in which only heads of households could vote. After the franchise reforms of 1918 and 1928 the system embraced most of the adult population. If it wished to be regarded as a credible mass party, aspiring to office, it could no longer afford to represent a class (as it clearly had done before the First World War); it had to offer itself as a party of broad appeal that cut across socio-economic divides. For true socialists, the question of holding office has always been less important than that of maintaining basic principles intact. Indeed, to the extent that government involves compromise, socialists have regarded it with deep suspicion, and have certainly been opposed to the adulteration of pure doctrine in the interests of popular support.

The events of 1931 served merely to confirm their worst fears in this respect, and the achievements (such as they were) of the governments of 1945–51 emphasised the same lesson. After Labour's defeat in the 1951 general election (a defeat which was technical, because Labour obtained more votes than the Conservatives, though fewer seats), socialists believed that Labour's industrial and welfare legislation would be repealed by the incoming Conservative government, that the policy of full employment would be abandoned, and that the resulting social turmoil would lead to the return of a Labour government in a few years' time. Of course this did not happen. Labour lost the two following general elections (1955 and 1959) by ever-widening margins. Socialists declared this was because the party was not radical enough. Social democrats—then known as Revisionists—

responded with a plea for doctrinal reform in the interests of popular appeal.

In the light of the split in the Labour Party following the defeat of 1979, the bitter disputes of the 1950s between Revisionists and socialists have an added significance; we can see, in these disputes, the emergence of a clear fault-line in the geology of the party. The socialists found a champion in Aneurin Bevan, possibly the only leader of stature that British socialism has ever produced. Bevan harried the Labour leadership on a number of foreign-policy and defence issues, such as German rearmament and nuclear weapons, but was unable to prevent the election of Hugh Gaitskell as leader in succession to Attlee in 1955. Gaitskell had many weaknesses as a leader: he was aloof, lacking in oratorical powers and in political craftsmanship—but he had closely studied the British electorate and he had come to the conclusion that it no longer wanted what socialism had to offer.

As early as August 1947 Gaitskell had confided to his diary that many Labour MPs representing marginal seats grossly misinterpreted the supposedly left-wing character of those who had elected them; the mass of the people, he observed, were 'very much against austerity, utterly uninterested in nationalisation of steel'. The three defeats of the 1950s led him to broaden this view; he came to the conclusion that the mixed economy was here to stay, that further public ownership was not wanted by the electors as a whole, and that the party he led had better come clean on these issues by agreeing to alter Clause 4 of its constitution:

Insofar as Labour appears to be doctrinaire on the subject of ownership [Gaitskell told the 1960 party conference], it saddles itself with a liability . . . [Clause 4] implies that we propose to nationalise everything, but do we? Everything?—the whole of light industry, the whole of agriculture, all the shops—every little pub and garage? Of course not. We have long ago come to accept, we know very well, for the foreseeable future, at least in some form, a mixed economy.

This attack upon nationalisation struck many within the party as rank heresy. At the 1957 party Conference Shinwell had declared public ownership to be 'the vital principle on which this party was founded'—a claim which was patently untrue, and as absurd as Bevan's claim three years earlier that 'the majority of people in Great Britain' deeply resented the establishment of the South-East Asia Treaty Organisation.

Gaitskell's attempt to alter Clause 4 was bolstered by the knowledge that a number of academic studies of voters' attitudes had demonstrated how unpopular nationalisation had become. Moreover, this research had been taken up by a group of younger party thinkers, prominent among whom were Anthony Crosland, Douglas Jay, Roy Jenkins and Denis Healey. The most erudite and hardest-hitting synthesis of their views came in 1956, with the publication of Crosland's *The Future of Socialism*. Crosland methodically demonstrated how radical had been the changes in British society since the 1930s; how, in particular, the achievement of full employment and the popularity of the welfare state had banished much of the poverty that had been the bleakest feature of pre-war Britain, and how the public ownership of basic industries had had so little to do with the prosperity that the nation now enjoyed. Was nationalisation an end in itself, or merely a means to an end? Crosland had no hesitation in answering that it was merely a device, a way of achieving greater social equality and of distributing national wealth more evenly.

In this work, and others (such as *The Conservative Enemy*, published in 1962) Crosland set out the prospectus for social democracy within the Labour Party: the socialist left was fighting yesterday's battles, using strategies based on a British society that no longer existed; social justice could be achieved without a great deal of public ownership, simply through the wise planning and regulation of the mixed economy which the country seemed to favour, assisted, certainly, by further reform of the nation's education system.

It is fair to say that the Revisionists were also more interested than the socialists in the pursuit of office. They failed to obtain an alteration of Clause 4, but when the socialists succeeded (1960) in persuading the party Conference to embrace unilateral nuclear disarmament, the Revisionists fought hard and successfully to have the policy reversed (1961), knowing how unpopular such a policy would be with the electorate. To assist their anti-socialist campaign the Revisionists formed the Campaign for Democratic Socialism (CDS), which included such figures as Crosland himself, Roy Jenkins and William Rodgers (then General Secretary of the Fabian Society), Christopher Mayhew and Reg Prentice. Mayhew later defected to the Liberal Party; Prentice joined the Conservatives and was given ministerial office by Mrs Thatcher in 1979, while Jenkins and Rodgers became founder-members of the Social Democratic Party (SDP) in 1981; it is reasonable to assume that Crosland—had he lived—would also have been an SDP adherent.

That the damaging rifts between socialists and Revisionists in the 1950s and early 1960s did not, at that time, lead to permanent schism was due to a combination of circumstances: Bevan's death in 1960, Gaitskell's in 1963, the growing troubles for the Conservative government, culminating in the Profumo affair (June 1963) and the unseemly public squabble for the Tory leadership following Macmillan's resignation a few months later. The Labour Party closed ranks behind Harold Wilson, who had managed to distance himself from the dogmatism of the Bevanites and who now attacked the Conservatives not for presiding over a capitalist society but for their incompetent management of it. In urging the party to 'unite on policy, not divide on theology', Wilson turned attention right away from unilateralism ('defence policy', he said, '. . . by the very nature of things changes from year to year and even from month to month'), and without for one moment suggesting that Clause 4 was somehow not quite right, he focused the mind of the party, and of the nation, upon 'the scientific revolution', promising (in the words of a 1963 party policy document) 'a new deal for the scientist and technologist in higher education, a new status for scientists in Government'.

The Wilson governments of 1964–70 were reformist, up to a point, but they were in no sense socialist. Gaitskellites were given important Cabinet positions, while left-wingers were neutralised in posts from which their impact on domestic policy was bound to be minimal: Barbara Castle in the Ministry of Overseas Development, Anthony Greenwood in the Colonial Office, Frank Cousins in the newly created Ministry of Technology. The one Bevanite to be given a significant domestic portfolio was Richard Crossman, who took charge of Housing & Local Government. The government's general economic strategy was thoroughly orthodox, incorporating tough restrictions on hire-purchase and local-authority borrowing, and a National Board for Prices & Incomes with a former Conservative MP and Minister, Aubrey Jones, at its head.

In 1966, following its defeat of a seamen's strike, the administration introduced a six-month freeze on wages and salaries. There was some extension of public ownership (the iron and steel industry was re-nationalised in 1967 and the National Freight Corporation was established the following year), but the major intervention in industry came with the setting-up of the Industrial Reorganisation Corporation (1966), to encourage mergers between private corporations through the provision of taxpayers' money — that is, helping capitalism to become stronger and more efficient. In 1969 Barbara Castle (now Secretary of State for Employment & Productivity) attempted to legislate to compel trade unions to observe 'cooling-off' periods before strikes or lock-outs could take legal effect, and to remove the legal immunity enjoyed by unofficial strikes. Although approved by the Commons these proposals were rejected by the Labour Party's National Executive Committee and the TUC. The legislation was abandoned. In June 1970 Wilson went to the country and was narrowly defeated.

The experience of 1964–70 had a profound effect on Labour. It distanced the party from the trade-union movement and led trade unionists to become disenchanted with parliamentary politics. This mood led inexorably to outright defiance by the TUC of the

Conservatives' 1971 Industrial Relations Act and contributed, in some measure, to the worsening record of labour disputes during Edward Heath's period as Prime Minister (June 1970–February 1974). Trade unionists ceased to have much confidence in politicians; they relied instead on their industrial muscle. The lesson which the left drew was not dissimilar: Labour Cabinets could not be trusted to pursue socialist policies, and Labour MPs could not, except under extreme duress, be trusted to oppose Labour Cabinets intent on ignoring party policy.

During this period the evidence of a revolt by the electorate against those things which socialists held most dear grew ever more formidable. The British Election Study team at Essex found that, among Labour identifiers, the proportion of voters favouring more nationalisation fell from 57 per cent (1964) to 50 per cent (February 1974); those wanting more spending on the social services fell from 89 per cent to 61 per cent over the same period; and those expressing general satisfaction with the power wielded by trade unions fell from 59 per cent to 44 per cent.[1] There is every indication that the attitudes typified in these responses hardened during the 1970s, more especially during the lifetime of the minority or near-minority Labour governments of 1974–9.

These governments, led first by Harold Wilson and then, from April 1976, by Jim Callaghan, negotiated a conclusion to the miners' strike that had precipitated the end of the Heath government, repealed the 1971 Industrial Relations Act and settled (by referendum) the dispute about Britain's membership of the Common Market. But inflation reached double figures (26 per cent by July 1975) and unemployment continued to grow; 5.9 per cent of the workforce were unemployed in the winter of 1977–8. Nor had there been any noticeable redistribution of the country's wealth; nearly one-third of all personal wealth was owned by 1 per cent of the population.

The rising tide of inflation and the worsening unemployment situation had a predictable effect on the international value of the pound, which on 27 October 1976 reached its lowest level yet against the dollar—$1.56 (though it was to fall to $1.09 under Mrs Thatcher). To help break the inflationary cycle that had been triggered by massive increases in oil and world commodity prices, and accelerated by the attempts of union pay negotiators to maintain living standards, the government tried to persuade the unions to agree to a voluntary wages policy—a £6 per week limit on all pay increases in 1975–6, and a 5 per cent limit, up to a maximum of £4 per week, in 1976–7. In July 1977, under Phase III of its incomes policy, the government imposed on the public sector a limit of 10 per cent for 1977–8, and announced that government contracts and assistance would not be given to firms in the private sector that broke this barrier; in 1978–9 this limit was to be 5 per cent—a policy repudiated by the Labour Party Conference on 2 October 1978.

Public-sector workers, encouraged by militant socialists, had already shown signs of stubborn resistance to these restrictions on free collective bargaining. The Glasgow dustmen's strike of 1975 and the prolonged nationwide firemen's strike in 1977–8 were preludes to the 'Winter of Discontent' (1978–9), when patients were refused admission to hospital and the dead went unburied. By the time of the May 1979 general election that brought Callaghan's government to an end, over a third of Labour voters (according to a BBC/Gallup poll) indicated their approval of the idea that families of strikers should be denied social security payments; nearly two-thirds supported legal regulation of trade-union activities; and 83.4 per cent expressed themselves in favour of a legal ban on secondary picketing—that is, picketing carried out at premises and against employers not directly involved in a dispute.

Throughout the 1970s, therefore, Labour's own supporters were voicing growing scepticism towards what had traditionally been regarded as essential parts of the Labour ethos: the extension of public ownership, more spending on the welfare state and the maintenance of trade-union power. A party that set its sights firmly on the acquisition of power would have taken due note of these trends, and trimmed its sails accordingly. But the move away from socialism on the part of its *supporters* was accompanied by a move in the opposite direction among its *activists*, whose influence within the party's policy-making structures grew more pervasive. They were able to do this because of the peculiar constitutional arrangements within the party, which had remained virtually unchanged since 1918.

The Conservative Party is, to be sure, a party of mass membership, but the mass membership's role in policy formation is, at best, purely consultative. What is termed by the media the Conservative 'Annual Conference' is really nothing more than the annual conference of the National Union, a sort of supporters' club to which local constituency parties send representatives. Power within the party—above all the power to make policy—is deliberately concentrated at the centre, and is largely in the hands of the Leader. The Conservative Annual Conference is heavily stage-managed, and although, on rare occasions, the 'rank-and-file' shows itself in a rebellious mood (usually over populist issues such as hanging), most of the time it remains docile and submissive.

The Labour Party is very differently organised. In 1918 a mass membership derived through constituency parties was added to the old federal structure of the LRC. The constituency parties and the affiliated bodies, of which the vast majority are trade unions, send delegates to the Annual Conference, which is—in theory— the supreme policy-making organ of the party. When Conference is not in session the party is controlled by its National Executive Committee (NEC). The composition of the NEC has undergone a number of changes since 1918, but some basic principles have remained intact. Foremost among these is the precept that, for elections to the NEC, as in the Conference as a whole, the trade unions have a predominating influence, for two reasons: the party was founded as and is still the political arm of the trade-union movement; and it is trade-union money that keeps the party alive.

By the 1970s the NEC had a membership of 29. Twelve of these were elected directly by the trade unions, and seven by the constituency parties; the Young Socialists and the co-operative societies elected one member each, and the Leader, Deputy Leader and party Treasurer sat on the NEC ex-officio; five women's representatives were also elected. In practice this constitutional arrangement meant that the unions controlled the election of a clear majority of the NEC—the twelve whom they directly selected, the five women and the Treasurer. Moreover, because of the operation of the block vote, whereby voting strength at Conference is determined by total membership of each affiliated organisation, the largest trade unions inevitably dominate. In 1982, when the cumulative total of the memberships of each affiliate came to 6,950,000, over two-thirds of this cumulative total were supplied by just the ten largest unions: the Railwaymen, the Electricians, the Communication [Post Office] Workers, the Construction Workers, Mineworkers, Shop Workers, Public Employees, General & Municipal Workers, Engineers and (largest of all, with a paper membership of 1.25 million) the Transport & General Workers.

We noted earlier that the apparatus of the block vote was originally introduced by the TUC in order to diminish socialist influence in its deliberations. Its importation into the Labour Party has had the opposite effect. It was the election of Frank Cousins as General Secretary of the Transport Workers in 1956 that had such a destabilising influence upon Gaitskell's leadership of the party; Cousins was a unilateralist, who at the 1960 party Conference swung his union's massive block vote behind a resolution completely rejecting 'any defence policy based on the threat of the use of strategic or tactical nuclear weapons'.

It is possible to justify the block vote on the grounds that the winner-takes-all principle is precisely that used at Westminster: the party that commands a majority of seats assumes power, irrespective of its popular support. None the less, objectively viewed, the block vote is a corrupt and corrupting influence. To begin with, the membership figures on the basis of which unions claim to cast block votes of particular size are often artificial and sometimes heavily massaged. The actual size of the block vote ought to reflect the number of union members who choose to pay the political levy. Since 1946 the law has assumed that all members of a union affiliated to the Labour Party will wish to pay the levy unless they positively indicate otherwise ('contract out'); given what we know about the changing political loyalties of trade unionists, this assumption would seem to be totally unwarranted. Many union workers are apparently unaware that they pay the levy at all.[2] At party Conferences the block vote cannot be split, to reflect, perhaps, a genuine division within the membership of a union on a particular issue. Finally, the membership levels at which unions affiliate seem to be influenced by ulterior motives, such as the need to generate more income for the party and the desirability of increasing the strength of the block vote for purely political ends.

It is questionable, therefore, whether the 600 or so delegations who make up the party Conference actually represent the views of those who pay the party membership fee. But one other feature of the party's constitutional structure deserves notice, namely the marginal role given to Labour MPs—the Parliamentary Labour Party (PLP). The PLP is not separately represented at Conference, and has no formal role on the NEC. It is true that since 1945 over half the NEC have been MPs, and that the constituency parties and the women's section habitually elect MPs to it. But these MPs represent those who have elected them, not the PLP as a whole. This situation reflects the view—also dating from the moment of the Labour Party's birth—that Labour MPs are nothing more than servants of the mass movement, elected to Westminster to do its bidding and to carry out its instructions; and if this holds good for Labour MPs, how much more so must it be true of the Labour Leader?

Viewed from the perspective of the British constitution, and of the conventions that protect it, the Labour Party is an anomaly. The party has always paid lip-service to the doctrine of accountability and to the concept of 'intra–party democracy': persons join the party and pay a membership fee; through a network of committees they elect delegates to the Annual Conference, which lays down policy; it is the duty of the NEC and of party members, including MPs, to see that these policy decisions are carried out, whether Labour is in opposition or in government. In 1937 Attlee put the matter thus: Conference 'lays down the policy of the party and issues *instructions* which must be carried out by the Executive, the affiliated organisations *and its representatives in Parliament* and on local authorities'.[3] By this view, MPs are bound to carry out Conference decisions. On issues of conscience some latitude is allowed. Otherwise they must do as Conference dictates.

The corollary of this view is that, when Labour is in power, the ultimate source of authority in the nation would not reside in Parliament, but in the NEC and the Annual Conference of the party. Such a scenario is of course at fundamental variance with the accepted view (derived from Edmund Burke) that an MP is a free agent, elected to the House of Commons to do whatever he feels to be in the national interest. In 1909 Lord Justice Farewell quoted Burke with approval when he dismissed, in the famous Osborne judgement, the claim of the Amalgamated Society of Railway Servants that it had a right to collect an annual sum from its members to provide for the representation of railwaymen in the Commons, on condition that MPs so sponsored accepted the Labour whip. An MP, he held, 'cannot be deprived of his independence, nor can he free himself from the great duty to the country that he undertakes by becoming a member'.

How has Labour been able to accommodate itself to the constitutional norms? The answer is that its leaders have ignored the rules by which the party is supposed to be bound. As early as 1907 Keir Hardie declared that members of the PLP could not be tied down by Conference motions. Attlee, as party leader both in opposition and in government, paid no attention to the doctrine of intra-party democracy that he had defined so closely in 1937, and both he and Wilson and Callaghan even set aside the procedure, drawn up after the events of 1931, by which a Labour Prime Minister is supposed to consult backbenchers and the party Secretary on whom to include in his Cabinet. In 1960 Gaitskell nearly came to grief over the unilateralist motion carried by Conference against his wishes, and the wishes of a majority of the PLP. But a nasty constitutional crisis was averted by the reversal of this policy a year later. In this episode, Gaitskell was able to use the considerable prestige and authority of the PLP, whose members had elected him as their Leader; the office of Leader of the *Party* did not exist until 1978.

In short, prior to 1970 the constitution of the Labour Party worked because for most of the time there was a gentlemen's agreement to leave well alone. After 1974 this concordat fell apart. The pretexts for its collapse were provided by some aspects of the history of the party in the 1970s, which must here be briefly sketched in.

After Labour's defeat in 1970 Conference became progressively less accommodating to the leadership. In part, especially during the years in opposition (1970–4), this was due to an entirely predictable alienation of the trade-union movement, in whose collective mouth a nasty taste had been left by the attempt to apply legislative shackles in 1969. Frank Cousins' leadership of the Transport & General Workers had already made it a less reliable supporter of the 'platform', and the replacement of the moderate Lord Carron by Hugh Scanlon as President of the Amalgamated

Union of Engineering Workers in 1967 signalled the fact that the destinies of the two largest affiliated unions (commanding, between them, almost a third of the Conference vote) were now firmly in left-wing hands. Wilson's decision to seek entry into the Common Market (vetoed by de Gaulle in November 1967) had further outraged trade-union feeling. British trade unionism has always been notoriously insular; the Common Market was regarded as nothing more than a club to further the interests of international capitalism. In October 1971 the Labour Conference decisively rejected entry on the terms negotiated by the Conservatives.

Meanwhile, a series of working parties had been set up to draft a new party programme, which was presented to and approved by Conference in October 1973. *Labour's Programme for Britain* was arguably the most socialist policy document to emerge from the party since 1918. In asserting that the aim of the party was to 'bring about a fundamental and irreversible shift in the balance of power and wealth in favour of working people and their families', Labour at last took on board the socialist objective of acquiring 'a major public stake in manufacturing industry'. Powers were to be taken by a future Labour administration to enable the state to take control of private companies. There was to be a programme of 'joint control' of firms, permitting trade-union involvement in the running of companies; the unions themselves were to be given statutory rights to information from and recognition by private employers.

These policies amounted to a clear rejection of the Revisionist approach. But the Wilson and Callaghan governments of 1974–9 did not in practice follow them. Faced with the most severe problems of a balance of payments deficit, galloping inflation and a militant (but not, so far as its mass membership was concerned, noticeably more socialist) trade-union movement, the governments fell back on the old deflationary orthodoxies (to which a new one, that of placing 'cash limits' on the spending of government departments, was added), pleading that these measures were necessary in order to obtain loans from the International Monetary Fund. These developments had a critical effect on the relationship between the Cabinet and the NEC, which neither Wilson nor Callaghan seemed able to control. Tony Benn, though a member of the Cabinet, used his influence on the NEC to campaign against Britain's continued membership of the Common Market; 18 NEC members made known their support for a 'No' vote in the 1975 referendum on this issue. The NEC also set its face against the exposure of alleged Trotskyist infiltration of the party, endorsed the appointment of Andy Bevan (a known Trotskyist) as the Party's Youth Officer, and signified its approval of the selection of Jimmy Reid as prospective Labour candidate at Dundee; Reid, a party member for only eight months at the time of his selection, had fought Central Dunbartonshire as a Communist in 1974.

The final months of the Callaghan administration witnessed a confrontation of unparalleled ferocity between the parliamentary leadership on the one hand and the socialist-controlled NEC and party Conference on the other. Conference, as already noted, rejected the 5 per cent pay limit. Callaghan retaliated by using powers implicit in Clause 5 of the party Constitution (according to which the contents of the election manifesto had to be agreed between the NEC and the parliamentary leadership) to veto the inclusion in the manifesto on which Labour fought the 1979 general election of a number of socialist propositions, such as a wealth tax, the abolition of the House of Lords, powers to freeze prices and to direct private enterprise, and more public expenditure to stimulate reflation.

The Labour Party has never recovered from the effects of this battle of wills. Callaghan was reported to have been very pleased at the dilutions he was able to achieve; Labour lost the 1979 election, but the centre-right of the PLP were probably justified in arguing that, had the manifesto not been watered down, the scale of defeat might have been that much greater. For the socialists, however, this was essentially a matter of secondary importance. Less concerned (as we have seen) with the practicalities of gaining power than with the principles by which they lived, they at once mounted a campaign the ultimate objective of which was to change the character of the party, and the personnel of the PLP, so that both would henceforth conform to a specifically socialist model.

In tracing the events that culminated in the constitutional reforms of 1980–1 chroniclers have inevitably concentrated on 'the left', and some have seen sinister, anti-democratic influences at work. According to one widely accepted view, between 1973 and 1981 'small groups of activists sought to change the Labour Party's constitution in order to secure *their own policies*'.[4] These activists (it is argued) had already gained great influence over Conference and, as a result, controlled the NEC; the betrayals of socialism perpetrated by Wilson, Callaghan and the moderate-dominated PLP had convinced the left that the policy-making process would have to be brought more fully under NEC control, and that steps would have to be taken to ensure that those selected as parliamentary candidates could be relied upon to accept the supremacy of Conference decisions.

Wilson's peremptory rejection of one of the central planks in Labour's 1973 *Programme*, the nationalisation of no less than 25 of the largest companies, appears to have been the spur to the formation of the Campaign for Labour Party Democracy (CLPD). The founding fathers and mothers of the CLPD were all Labour Party members; those whom they recruited, such as the MPs Joan

Maynard, Jo Richardson, Ernie Wise and Neil Kinnock, belonged to the respectable, parliamentary left, and followed in the Bevanite socialist tradition. Adherents of the CLPD shared a strong antipathy to the Common Market and to nuclear weapons, and they believed that no Labour Party could flourish that did not have strong links with the trade-union movement. They embraced a vision of a socialist Britain that excluded the revisionism of Gaitskell and Crosland and, in consequence, the idea of a mixed economy. Most of all, however, members of the CLPD took seriously—indeed, literally,—not merely the wording of Clause 4 of the Labour Party's constitution (the clause printed on the party's membership card) but also the supremacy of Conference and Conference decisions, which in their view the members of the PLP were bound to follow.

Viewed from an historical perspective, these convictions were entirely within the Labour tradition; there was nothing extremist or revolutionary about them. Both the CLPD and the more policy-orientated Labour Co-ordinating Committee (the LCC, formed 1978, and concerned largely with economic and industrial policy and withdrawal from the Common Market) utterly rejected extra-parliamentary means of achieving a socialist state; indeed, the criticism can be levelled at them that they concerned themselves excessively with the chain of command within the Labour Party, and not sufficiently with the relationship between the party and the electorate.

Members of the CLPD and the LCC declared themselves adherents of the 'Outside Left', but only to distinguish themselves from 'Inside Left' organisations, such as the well-established Tribune Group. Tribune is a parliamentary presssure group, a club of left-wing MPs who have never attempted to set up an extra-parliamentary arm involving trade unions or constituency parties. The CLPD and the LCC, which joined forces in 1980 with the Socialist Campaign for Labour Victory and the Militant Tendency under the banner of the Rank and File Mobilising Committee (RFMC), all believed strongly in the efficacy of nationwide campaigns to convert the unions and the constituency parties not so much to a particular brand of socialism as to a particular view of the relationship between the PLP and the party Conference.

Members of the Tribune Group, and those within the party who supported them, deferred to the parliamentary leadership, giving that leadership the benefit of the doubt when questions of policy were at issue. There was nothing deferential about the Outside Left, which openly and unashamedly began to win for its adherents positions of influence and authority in union branches and constituency Labour parties. Creeping disillusion with the record of the Wilson and Callaghan governments of 1974–9 boosted the popularity of Outside Left policies, prominent among which was the demand that every Labour MP should be obliged to submit him or herself for reselection at least once in the lifetime of a Parliament.

The object behind mandatory reselection was of course to make every Labour MP more accountable to the local constituency party, and more aware of the need to do what the constituency party wanted, rather than follow the dictates of his or her own conscience or the wishes of the party leadership. Under a system of mandatory reselection (it was argued), Labour MPs would constantly feel the breath of the constituency parties down their necks. This would act as a wonderful corrective to the influence and patronage of the leadership; indeed, truly socialist MPs would welcome the protection it afforded against the atmosphere of compromise that seemed to infect the corridors of Westminster.

The campaign for mandatory reselection gathered momentum in the wake of the controversies surrounding Dick Taverne (1973), Eddie Griffiths (1974), Reg Prentice (1975) and Frank Tomney (1976). Taverne, a pro-Marketeer, had a vote of no confidence passed on him by the CLP at Lincoln, but continued to sit as Social Democratic MP from 1973 to 1974, when Labour lost the seat. Griffiths (Sheffield Brightside), Prentice (Newham North-East) and Tomney (Hammersmith North) were all refused readoption after having fallen foul of socialist-dominated constituency parties. In 1978 the question of mandatory reselection was raised at the party Conference, but owing to the forgetfulness of Hugh Scanlon, who failed to cast the Engineers' one million votes in its favour, the motion was lost. Its passage in 1979, after Labour had been voted out of office and in the mood of anger at the 'betrayal' of socialist principles by the Callaghan government, was assured.

Mandatory reselection obliges incumbent Labour MPs to submit themselves for readoption within three years of a general election; they can no longer count on being reselected automatically. In the short term its effect has hardly been dramatic. Betwen the elections of 1979 and 1983 a grand total of eight Labour MPs were refused adoption, while another nine who would probably have suffered this fate defected to the SDP; if we add to these figures a handful of MPs (such as Bob Mellish) who retired under threat of deselection, we might be justified in concluding that about 20 Labour MPs suffered directly or indirectly from the new procedure. Between 1983 and 1987 a further six Labour MPs suffered deselection; two of these (Norman Atkinson at Tottenham and Ernie Roberts at Hackney North) were ousted in order to make way for Black candidates (respectively Bernie Grant and Diane Abbott). Again, there were also a number of enforced retirements, notably John Silkin at Deptford and Reg Freeson (to make way for Ken Livingstone) at Brent East.

Mandatory reselection by itself, therefore, cannot be said to have played a major part in the battle of left against right in the party. It is undeniable, however, that in the longer term the psychological impact of mandatory reselection is likely to be very significant indeed, for its institution has strengthened the position of the constituency Labour party in its relationship with its Labour MP, and is bound to result in the attraction as would-be Labour MPs of those who are readier to see themselves not as representatives in the Burkeian sense, but as delegates of the local party machine. This is likely to strengthen the influence of socialism within the party as a whole.

For all that has been asserted about the influence of the Outside Left in bringing about constitutional change within the party, mandatory reselection was its only complete victory. Another of its ambitions was to wrest control of the party manifesto away from the Leader and deliver it into the hands of the NEC. Callaghan's refusal to include abolition of the House of Lords (which had become official party policy) in the 1979 manifesto was cited in support of this ambition, but it has remained unfulfilled. At the 1979 Conference an instruction to the NEC to bring forward proposals designed to ensure that it 'alone, after the widest possible consultation with all sections of the movement, would take the final decision as to the contents of the Labour Party general election manifesto' was passed by the comparatively small majority of 800,000 votes. But at the Blackpool Conference of 1980 the proposals which the NEC dutifully presented were lost by 117,000 votes, largely as a result of last-minute faint-heartedness on the part of some trade-union delegations.

The quest for a more democratic way of electing the party Leader was more complicated. We have already noted that, until 1978, there was no such office as 'Leader' of the party as a whole, only Leader of the PLP, elected by the PLP. The election, by Labour MPs, of Callaghan as Wilson's successor in April 1976 dismayed the left. That election marked the first occasion on which the PLP had chosen a Leader while in office and, in fact, was the first occasion on which a Prime Minister had been elected, by his parliamentary colleagues, to that position. After three ballots Callaghan won against Michael Foot by 176 votes to 137. The Outside Left argued that the PLP had not reflected, in this choice, the views of the party faithful. They also pointed out that in 1976 the Liberal Party had changed its method of electing the Liberal Leader, so that every Liberal Party member had a vote, although the choice had to be confined to Liberal MPs.

There was widespread agreement within the Labour Party that it should have a Leader, and that the Leader should be elected by a mechanism that involved all sections of the membership. There was no agreement as to how this mechanism should be constructed. Ideally, the CLPD would have wanted the Leader to be elected by Conference as a whole; but Conference is, as we have seen, dominated by a few large trade unions, and the fickleness of some union leaders led to a modification of the purist notion of the sovereignty of Conference decisions. In any case, the possibility was now raised of a clash between the party and the PLP, because in terms of Conference proceedings the PLP is numerically powerless. The CLPD therefore acquiesced in the idea of an electoral college in which, in the form finally approved by a special Conference held at Wembley in January 1981, the trade unions have 40 per cent of the votes, and the PLP and the constituency parties 30 per cent each.

At the time the institution of the electoral college was seen as further proof of the incompatibility of a socialist-dominated Labour Party and the British constitution. What would happen (it was asked) if, supposing Labour were in power, the electoral college chose as Leader an MP whose authority the PLP refused to accept? Might this not place the Queen in a difficult position, since her constitutional duty is to summon, to form a government, an MP who can command a majority *in the Commons*? Might there not, in effect, then be *two* Labour Leaders, one having the backing of the mass party and another enjoying the support merely of the Labour parliamentarians? Do not dilemmas of this sort prove, somehow, that Labour is not a party 'fit to govern'?

Leaving aside the fact that difficulties of this kind could equally conceivably arise over the leadership of the Democrats, and the fact that objections of this sort were not raised in May 1940, when Winston Churchill became Prime Minister but the man he replaced, Neville Chamberlain, remained Conservative Party Leader until the following October, we need to look at how Labour's electoral college has actually worked since its inception.

Callaghan's expected resignation, and his replacement as Leader by Michael Foot (October–November 1980) took place before the electoral college was instituted. It first came into operation on 27 September 1981 for the election of Deputy Leader. This contest revolved around the candidatures of Denis Healey, the former Chancellor of the Exchequer whose policies had been the target of so much socialist criticism, and Tony Benn, the former peer who, as a member of the Labour governments of 1974–9, had used his position on the NEC to try to win, at Conference, some of the battles he lost in Cabinet. In popular mythology Benn was closely associated with the constitutional changes of 1979–81. In fact, he was careful not to jump on that particular bandwagon until after Labour's 1979 defeat, when he joined the CLPD and, in 1980, associated himself with the Rank and File Mobilising Committee.

Benn's socialist credentials were, of course, beyond reproach; but his apparent willingness to work with the non-parliamentary left was an embarrassing reminder of Labour's Marxist origins.

In the Deputy Leadership contest Benn was the candidate of the Outside Left, Healey of the revisionist right. The Inside Left salved its conscience by prevailing upon the respectable Tribunite John Silkin to declare himself a candidate also. Silkin came bottom of the poll on the first ballot, and on the second, in a straight fight with Benn, Healey secured victory by the narrowest of margins: 0.852 per cent of the electoral college votes. It was at once apparent that Healey's success had been due in part to the deliberate abstention of 37 members of the Tribune Group of MPs, including Joan Lestor and Neil Kinnock. When the electoral college was again brought into use (October 1983) following Michael Foot's resignation, it was Kinnock who emerged victorious, securing a massive 71 per cent of the electoral college votes and easily beating off challenges from Peter Shore and Eric Heffer; the victory of Kinnock's moderate running-mate, Roy Hattersley, as Deputy Leader, was just as convincing.

The constitutional changes by themselves have, therefore, had only a limited impact upon Labour's public face. What has undoubtedly had a much more profound effect is the public perception of the party as one manipulated by sinister forces, exploiting apathy and weakness within the lowest echelons of the party structure in order to transform it into something other than that which its membership has (so the argument goes) traditionally desired.

The Labour Party has never been able to break completely free from the umbilical cord that tied it, as the very moment of its birth, to revolutionary socialism. Nor has it ever been able to cast aside the equally strong tradition of 'extra-parliamentary' activity, ranging from mass lobbying and marching through 'civil disobedience' to outright defiance of the law. In the 1980s a number of Labour-controlled local authorities, such as Liverpool, Sheffield, Lambeth, Camden and Islington, tried to flout (and for a time succeeded in flouting) Conservative legislation on rate-capping by simply refusing to set a legal rate. Many of the councillors concerned, such as Derek Hatton, the former Deputy Leader in Liverpool, have since been surcharged and disqualified. Neil Kinnock has neither defended them nor undertaken, should Labour return to power at Westminster, to remove these penalties.

But it is they, not Kinnock, who have acted in the Labour tradition. In 1921 George Lansbury, the Labour leader of Poplar Borough Council, together with 29 other Poplar councillors, spent 41 days in prison for refusing to agree to the payment of an excessive rate to the Conservative-controlled London County Council. 'Poplarism', as it became known, was a protest against the inequitable rate burden then falling down upon the poor compared with the wealthier London boroughs, and was in turn part of a wider campaign to raise the level of Poor Law payments to the needy of London's East End. The young Clement Attlee fully supported Lansbury's action, and associated himself with demands that the disqualifications imposed upon Lansbury and his colleagues be removed (which they were). But no one accused Attlee of being a Trotskyist anti-democratic revolutionary. Nor, after the 1950 general election, was the Conservative Party similarly accused when it urged the privately owned iron and steel industry not to co-operate in implementing the Nationalisation Act passed by Labour the previous year, in the hope that a further general election soon expected would result in a Conservative government that would repeal the 1949 legislation. People have forgotten events such as these, or else have chosen not to remember them. Instead, the mind of the public has been focused upon the activities of a few extremist groups whose influence upon the broad thrust of Labour politics has been marginal, though admittedly well-publicised.

When the appeal to the revolutionary left of the Communist Party of Great Britain declined in the 1950s, as its Stalinist philosophy became internationally as well as nationally discredited, former or would-be adherents renewed, in a much more sympathetic light, their acquaintance with the ideas of Leon Trotsky, whom Stalin had had assassinated and who claimed to be Lenin's true disciple. British followers of Trotsky have never been able to unite in a single organisation; an attempt to establish 'Socialist Unity' at the time of the 1979 general election failed—as it was bound to. Partly as a result, in the 1980s some Trotskyist factions—notably the International Marxist Group and the Militant Tendency—advocated 'entryism'— joining the Labour Party in order to strengthen the hand of the parliamentary socialists; in practising this art, Militant (formed as long ago as 1950) has been most successful.

The constitution of the Labour Party forbids the affiliation of any organisation having its own programme, principles and policy, or having constituency branches, or putting up its own candidates at parliamentary or local-government levels, or 'owing allegiance to any political organisation situated abroad'. Militant could claim to have infringed none of these stipulations; its supporters merely sold a newspaper, *Militant*, and worked hard (which was undeniable) in support of constituency Labour parties, putting official party literature through letterboxes, canvassing assiduously, and turning up regularly, and in large numbers, to branch meetings. A more devoted group of party members was not to be found. By 1983 Militant supporters were well entrenched in the youth organisation of the Labour Party, and in some CLPs, notably in inner London, Bradford and Liverpool; at the 1983 election four of Labour's seven candidates in Liverpool were identified as Militant supporters.

The record of Militant Labour Party candidates has been mixed; but it cannot be said to have been uniformly bad. At Bradford North the adoption, after a protracted struggle, of Pat Wall led to a split in the party which caused the seat to be lost to the Conservatives; it was, however, recaptured, by Pat Wall, in 1987. At Liverpool Broadgreen, Terry Fields retained the seat in 1983 with the biggest increase in the Labour vote recorded in any constituency compared with 1979; in 1987 Fields' percentage of the total constituency vote expanded further, from 40.9 to 48.6 per cent. Another Militant supporter, Dave Nellist (Coventry South East) had fared badly in 1983 (retaining the seat on a Labour vote lower than in 1979 by over 11 per cent); but in 1987 Nellist pushed Labour's share of the vote up to 47.5 per cent.

Labour Party moderates have used the spectre of Militant as a scare tactic, and have led witch-hunts against Militant supporters (notably the expulsion by Conference in 1982 of five members of the *Militant* editorial board and, in 1986–7, of eleven leading Liverpool Militants, including Mr Hatton) as a useful diversionary tactic. It is worth recording that, in as much as Labour suffered in 1987 from its 'loony left' image, the major troublespots—such as the Labour-led GLC in its final years, and the London Borough of Brent—*cannot* be identified as Militant enclaves. At Brent much of the adverse publicity that Labour has attracted has arisen from the attempts of Black elements to push through ethnically orientated policies (such as the monitoring of schoolteachers) which are, in fact, anathema to Militant diehards. In Liverpool the refusal of Militant to espouse Black politics led to a public rift; the resultant bitterness can still be felt.

Militant believes in the necessity and in the reality of class struggle, and regards policies that (however well-intentioned) emphasise race—or sex—rather than class, as a betrayal of socialism. In London as a whole Labour's 1987 reverses cannot be blamed on Militant, though they might be laid at the door of the socialist left ('a greater danger than the Liverpool Militants ever were'[5]), whose takeover of the GLC and the ILEA in 1981 was followed by the capture of Camden, Greenwich, Hackney, Islington, Lewisham and Southwark in 1982, Brent, Ealing, Hammersmith and Waltham Forest in 1986, and Hounslow in 1987.

It has always suited the Conservatives to portray Labour as a Trojan horse, all the more dangerous because those who ride in it are often (it is said) blissfully unaware of the true nature of the beast that is carrying them. Labour moderates, in an effort to stem the tide of socialism in their party, have sometimes joined in this refrain. The reality of Labour's recent history is much simpler. Following the constitutional reforms of 1980–1, but due, also, to the persistent lobbying of socialist activists, and to their success in spreading their influence in trade-union branches and CLPs, the policies of the Labour Party became palpably more left wing. A cursory reading of the 1983 election manifesto confirms this view.

In 1983 Labour declared its readiness to 'expand the economy, by providing a strong and measured increase in public spending'; part of this increase was to result from higher taxes. 'Like any other expanding industrial enterprise', the 1983 manifesto explained, 'we shall borrow to finance our programme of investment . . . There is no shortage of savings available [an ominous phrase] for borrowing today.' Labour promised 'a new partnership' with the trade unions, the repeal of 'divisive Tory "employment" laws', and 'new statutory support for collective bargaining'. To prevent the expected rush of international money out of the British economy, exchange controls were to be reintroduced; a Price Commission was to be given powers to order price freezes and reductions. On public ownership, Labour warned that while multinational companies would be closely monitored, powers would be taken 'to invest in individual companies, to purchase them outright or to assume temporary control'; 'the public assets and rights hived off by the Tories' would be returned to public ownership, and a Labour government would 'establish a significant stake in electronics, pharmaceuticals, health equipment and building materials; and also in other important sectors, as required in the national interest'. All forms of academic selection in schools were to be prohibited; the charitable status enjoyed by private schools was to be brought to an end. Local authorities were to be empowered 'to repurchase homes sold under the Tories on first resale'. The House of Lords was to be abolished as quickly as possible; Ireland was to be unified 'by consent'; Britain was to be taken out of the Common Market; a non-nuclear defence policy was to be implemented in stages. Finally, the 1983 manifesto included a miscellany of provisions that reflected the power which certain sectional interests have been able to accrue in the wake of the socialist advance: the banning of various blood sports; protection for animals in zoos, circuses and safari parks; the establishment of a Palestinian state; and opposition to 'the Turkish junta'.

When Neil Kinnock assumed the leadership, he attempted to move the party from a left-wing to a more centrist position, as Harold Wilson had successfully done 20 years before. Like Wilson, Kinnock had an impressive left-wing pedigree. The son of a South Wales miner, he had been a member of CND and CLPD; he had opposed British membership of the EEC; and he had used his undoubted oratorical powers to harry the Wilson-Callaghan governments in the late 1970s, and to berate them for their lack of left-wing idealism. At the time of his election as Leader Kinnock (then aged 41) was identified with the Tribune Group; he was the acknowledged protégé of Michael Foot but, unlike Foot, he had become ambitious enough to see that the practicalities of winning power demanded that much of the left-wing ideological baggage needed to be either jettisoned or kept well out of sight. As we have noted, he was quick to distance himself from Tony Benn's challenge to Denis Healey for the Deputy Leadership in 1981 and, on becoming Leader himself, he initiated a thorough review of Labour policies, establishing a Campaign Strategy Committee as a counterweight to the NEC.

Kinnock was quite brazen in his view that, in projecting dogma without reference to realism, Labour had brought the disaster of 1983 upon itself; if it seriously wanted electoral success, it needed to address the voters in a language that they understood, and on issues which they considered important. This meant that policies would have to be evolved that made, at the very least, some acknowledgement of the aspirations of home-owners as well as of council-tenants; that recognised the unpopularity of public owner-ship and the support for secret trade-union ballots; and which accepted that the debate about EEC membership was over. The task of persuading the party to accept this approach was not easy. Kinnock's relationship with the NEC was frequently tense—no more so than over his insistence on the expulsion of the Liverpool Militants (March 1987)—and his measured denunciation of Arthur Scargill's conduct of the miners' strike was certainly not calculated to endear him to the hard left.

But, however frustrated the left may have been at the content and style of the Kinnock leadership, it had no alternative to offer. Tony Benn had failed to gain election to Parliament in 1983; he was unable to re-enter the Commons until returned at the Chesterfield by-election of March 1984. By then, Kinnock had managed to establish a firm hold on the party machine, taking advantage of the post-election disarray on the left and giving positions of responsi-bility to David Blunkett, leader of Sheffield City Council, and to Michael Meacher, Benn's former lieutenant. Kinnock was also careful to maintain good relations with the trade unions; he abandoned any talk of a statutory incomes policy under a future Labour government and (April 1985) promised to reduce unemployment by one million in his first two years as Prime Minister.

As newly elected Leader, Kinnock's honeymoon was unusually prolonged, partly because of extreme sensitivity within the party during the miners' strike and at the time of the reselection contests, and partly because of indications of growing party popularity, reflected especially in local-election successes in May 1985, when Labour regained control of Birmingham and, for the first time, won power in Edinburgh. The grave difficulties experienced by the Thatcher government during the Westland affair at the end of 1985 served also to strengthen Kinnock's hand in dealing with unruly elements. Certainly, in persuading the party to adopt a new set of policies on which to fight the next general election, Kinnock's difficulties were remarkably few.

But this tranquillity was paid for at a price, based upon the need to balance the demands of the electorate against internal party pressures. In 1987 Labour presented a set of themes that reflected some—but only some—recognition of the changing values of the British electorate. Sensing that wider share ownership through privatisation schemes was basically popular, Labour talked about 'social ownership', and warned that a future Labour government would take 'a socially owned stake in high-tech industries and other concerns'; private shares in British Telecom and British Gas would not be sequestered, but rather 'converted into special new securities'. Council-tenants wanting to buy their own homes were assured that this right would continue, and trade unionists were give to understand that Conservative legislation that had given them the right to decide, by secret ballot, whether or not to go on strike would remain intact. None the less, the 1987 manifesto made clear that Labour was committed to a massive extension of trade-union privileges (for instance, in the sphere of recognition by employers), and there was a specific commitment to reinstate miners unfairly dismissed. On defence policy the manifesto pro-claimed the need to 'end the nuclear pretence', and in the social sphere steps were to be taken 'to ensure that homosexuals are not discriminated against'.

Labour's 1987 offering was only half the size of the document set before the electorate in 1983. Conspicuous by their absence (compared with 1983) were any proposals to abolish the House of Lords, withdraw from the European Community, or shut down American nuclear bases in the UK. Yet the manifesto's lack of detail on such matters as nationalisation and taxation served to unnerve the more affluent voters rather than to reassure them. Labour's national popularity, as reflected in opinion-poll ratings, had peaked at almost 40 per cent in the summer of 1986; it then plummeted, disastrously, to around 32 per cent by the beginning of 1987. At the District Council elections on 8 May 1987 the Alliance gained ground at the expense of both major parties, but more so at Labour's expense than at that of the Tories. Labour entered the 1987 general election in incomparably better shape (in terms both of policy and of organisation) than it had been in 1983. Kinnock's ascendancy over and within it was total. But it was a party deeply distrusted by about two-thirds of the voting public.

Nationally, Neil Kinnock was seen as a warm and congenial figure, but lacking in qualities of leadership when compared with Mrs Thatcher, and even with David Steel and David Owen, the Alliance leaders. Kinnock's easy manner and personal charm did not and could not compensate for widespread opposition to

Labour's non-nuclear defence policy, with which he was personally identified. Nor did a majority of voters believe either that the nation's economic well-being would improve under Labour rule, or that it could safely be entrusted to Labour's care. Most of all, Labour was seen as a party that was both divisive and divided. The running battles between various factions of the left, exemplified in the refusal of the NEC to endorse Les Huckfield's candidature at Knowsley North (October–November 1986) and in the loss of Greenwich by the hard-left candidate. Deirdre Wood (February 1987), had had a predictable effect on the public's perception of Labour's alleged new-found unity. This perception had been affected—equally predictably—by the antics of 'loony left' Labour-controlled councils, especially in London. Voters who were charitable enough to forget Mr Kinnock's left-wing past, or to forgive him for it, saw him as 'a nice guy'—if anything, too nice. But the party he led was regarded as, at best, incompetent and unfit to govern.

Since the election defeat of 1987 Kinnock has taken further steps to steer the party in a 'centre-left' direction. His success has not been total. In the autumn of 1987 Conference backed his proposal for 'one-member-one-vote' (expressed through an electoral-college arrangement designed to maintain the participation of trade unions) in the selection and reselection of parliamentary candidates, thus removing the selection process from the constituency General Management Committees (which, popular wisdom had it, the hard left found easier to control) to the CLPs as a whole. Because this reform was opposed by some on the left, like Tony Benn, it was written up by the media as a weapon of the right. Nothing could be further from the truth. Among Kinnock's closest supporters in pushing through this reform was Ron Todd, general secretary of the TGWU and a man of unexceptionable left-wing credentials. The aim of 'one-member-one-vote' was to attempt to neutralise the power of unrepresentative extremists at constituency level, not to smother the influence of respectable socialists.

Much better indices of the balance of power between socialists and revisionists are offered by the state of the PLP, the Shadow Cabinet and the NEC. In July 1987 the PLP elected a new Shadow Cabinet: four moderates, including Peter Shore, were defeated while six left-wingers (Robin Cook, Jack Straw, Frank Dobson, Robert Hughes, Gordon Brown and Ms Jo Richardson) were voted on; John Prescott, another left-winger and a member of the outgoing team, moved into second place (behind Bryan Gould) and Michael Meacher into third. Labour's new front-bench team now has a left-wing majority. The following September the pro-Kinnock majority on the NEC was consolidated; but at the same time Ken Livingstone was elected on to the NEC, polling more votes than Bryan Gould, hailed as the architect of a new brand of 'designer socialism'.

Kinnock's hold on the party appeared to be strong, but he had, perforce, to lead it from a position far to the left of that occupied by Attlee or Wilson. These Leaders had once been of the left, but were able to pull themselves free; Kinnock, whether he likes it or not, is the left's prisoner. He managed to obtain Conference approval for a fundamental review of all aspects of policy, based on the recognition that if it is ever to win a general election Labour must advance in the South of England, where self-interest, not socialism, holds sway. Gould has urged that Labour must 'successfully appeal to those who want and enjoy rising living standards, who own or want to own their own homes . . . upward mobility is a very proper socialist objective . . . Instead of opposing wider share-ownership . . . we should set about making it a reality'; but he has also reassured the left that he remains committed to 'equality, to collective provision of important services . . . [and] . . . to a non-nuclear defence policy'.[6] Professor Ben Pimlott, a leading Labour intellectual, has warned that instead of grudgingly acknowledging the popularity of council-house sales Labour 'must think of ways of extending a manifest benefit to other would-be buyers'.[7]

If this outlook leads to a rejection of old-style nationalisation in favour of 'popular socialism', it is bound to lead to a further split in the party, which the present leadership will certainly wish to avoid. Clause 4 will therefore be preserved intact. Nor will it be easy to overturn Labour's commitment to non-nuclear defence, to which both Gould and Kinnock are in any case pledged (though with less enthusiasm than hitherto) and which was certainly Labour's greatest electoral liability in 1987. There is much trade-union opposition to wider share ownership, which is regarded as a means of frustrating 'workers' control'.

Labour's trade-union connections provide another source of electoral weakness. Union membership has contracted by over three million since 1979; only about 37 per cent of the British workforce are in trade unions now compared with 50 per cent when Mrs Thatcher first took office. But union assets have remained remarkably healthy—thanks partly to the boom in property values in the 1980s—and union support for Labour is as essential as ever. In some respects the unions have proved themselves indispensable allies in containing extremism. In October 1987 it was the block votes of the unions that ensured the defeat by Conference of motions calling for the creation of separate Black sections of the party. In December leading trade unionists in London announced their support for 'Labour First', a new national organisation founded to reduce the influence of the hard left in constituency parties in the capital and other major cities. Unions supported Kinnock's purge of the Young Socialists (November 1987) and the forcing out of Andy Bevan at the beginning of 1988.

Yet the public image of the unions is decidedly negative. The popular perception of trade unions as controlled by extremists and militants has remained strong; even among union members themselves almost half of a sample interviewed in August 1987 admitted to this view.[8] The capture of the TGWU by the hard left, which won control of its general executive council in February 1988, served as an embarrassing reminder that this perception is very well grounded; among those elected to the council was Mr Alan Quinn, a Militant supporter who in 1987 was actually elected to Labour's national constitutional committee that had been established to deal with Militant infiltration of the party!

The strategy of the present Labour leadership, the use of trade-union influence as a counter to political extremism in the constituencies, thus carries dangers of its own. Within the world of Labour policy-making, the unions have always exacted a price for their support and for their money. At the next general election this price is likely to include the scrapping of many of the Conservative government's trade-union reforms, such as the sequestration of assets and the banning of sympathy strikes and secondary industrial action. Such a package would certainly be popular with many unions; public reaction to such proposals is equally like to be very hostile.

The Benn-Heffer challenge to the Kinnock-Hattersley leadership in 1988 was equally unwelcome. In so far as the challenge was doctrinal, based (in Tony Benn's words) on the desire to 'offer members of the party and the affiliated unions an opportunity to choose a different course',[9] it only served to underline the dichotomous nature of the party, in which two dogmas struggle for mastery of its soul. Kinnock's victory (with 88.6 per cent of the votes) was comprehensive (though Hattersley's, at 66.8 per cent, was much less so), and it was inevitable that the Labour Leader would seek to use it as a springboard for carrying into effect the great review of policy initiated after the 1987 defeat. But what will be the political implications of such a review? A Labour Party which, at the next general election, offers nothing more than a version of Thatcherism will have a hard time convincing the electorate that it can be trusted to administer Conservative policies better than the Conservatives. Moreover, those who stayed with Labour in 1987 will be sorely tempted to abstain, and the abstentions may grow if unilaterialism is abandoned. A Labour Party that did not place a high priority upon the alleviation of poverty and an end to unemployment—both of which presuppose high taxation policies—would lack credibility in the eyes of those who have most loyally supported it hitherto.

The left will not allow any such policy changes to take place without a bitter struggle, in which its rock-solid belief that principles are more important than power will be pressed with all the force at its command. The left's growing faith in proportional representation (PR) is symptomatic of this outlook. In the past Labour has opposed PR because it would in all probability lead to coalition government and the politics of compromise. PR is now viewed as the best way of cutting Conservative strength in the Commons down to size. 'It's a sobering thought', Mineworkers' leader Arthur Scargill said in August 1987, 'that, had we had proportional representation, it's highly unlikely that Mrs Thatcher would be Prime Minister.'[10] PR would ensure an end to Conservative rule at a price—an end to Labour's hopes of forming a government on its own—which many on the left are now willing to pay. For Neil Kinnock this is of course a bleak prospect. But given the multiparty nature of British and especially of English politics, the most he can hope for in the 1990s is that the unity of Labour will be maintained in a degree sufficient for him to take office as part of a wider anti-Conservative coalition government.

NOTES

1. I. Crewe, B. Sarlvik & J. Alt, 'Partisan Dealignment in Britain, 1964–1974', *British Journal of Political Science*, vol. vii (1977).
2. M. Moran (1974), *The Union of Post Office Workers*, London, Macmillan, found that only half were so aware, and that only a fifth thought the union should affiliate to the Labour Party. The 1984 Trade Union Act requires unions to ballot their members on whether or not they wish to maintain a political fund.
3. C. Attlee (1937), *The Labour Party in Perspective*, London, Odhams, p. 93; the emphasis is mine.
4. D. and M. Kogan (1982), *The Battle for the Labour Party*, London, Fontana, p. 11; the emphasis is mine.
5. Anne Sofer in *The Times*, 10 May 1987.
6. *Sunday Times*, 27 September 1987.
7. *Sunday Times*, 5 July 1987.
8. MORI in *The Times*, 7 September 1987.
9. *The Times*, 24 March 1988.
10. *The Times*, 10 August 1987.

3. Liberal Democracy and Social Democracy

The constitutional upheaval experienced by Labour in the early 1980s had, as a direct outcome, a splintering away from the party of a group of anti-socialist (as opposed to non-socialist) revisionists, who for a time were able to operate as a 'fourth force' in English politics before agreeing, amid much acrimony, to merge with the Liberals. Both the Liberals and the Social Democrats operated on the periphery of the political scene. Given the very fluid state of politics in Britain in the 1970s and 1980s this periphery is not unimportant. Yet there is little evidence to support the hopes of those optimists who believe that a third force can operate on the centre of the political stage, or that parties that are now located on the margins can be re-established at the centre.

The modern Liberal Party has very little in common with the party of the same name led by Gladstone in the second half of the nineteenth century. Gladstonian Liberalism exhibited two outstanding characteristics: first, an unalterable belief in the value of free trade and an abhorrence of protective tariffs; second, a somewhat less entrenched conviction that the less the state interfered in the lives of its citizens, the better. Underlying both these views was a deep opposition to state-aided privilege, and this opposition sprang in turn from the experiences of those who, in 1859, came together to form the party.

The backbone of nineteenth-century Liberalism was provided by the bourgeoisie, the merchants and manufacturers who had made

Britain 'the workshop of the world'. Their faith in the justice of the market-place was apparently unshakeable, and to this end they favoured an economic policy that would make manufacturing and exporting as cheap as possible: no taxes on imports of raw materials; the encouragement of bilateral free-trade agreements with other countries; and no taxes on food, especially imported corn, so that wage-rates could be kept low. At the same time they supported the absence of state interference with manufacturing industry (in matters such as hours and conditions of work), and the muzzling of trade unions, the activities of which they regarded as a restraint on trade and an unnatural interference with the operation of the free market: the cure for unemployment was to be found in lower wages (leading to increased production) and emigration to the colonies.

'*Laissez-faire*' — leaving industry alone — could not survive the 1867 Reform Act, a Conservative measure that gave the vote to working-class male heads of households; in any case, *laissez-faire* had already been breached, in the case of women and children, by the factory reforms of the 1840s. The radical wing of the Liberal coalition gained a much stronger grip on the policy-making organs of the party in the 1880s, provoking a series of internal convulsions which culminated in the great split of 1886 over Irish Home Rule. In large measure the propertied classes deserted, via Liberal Unionism, to the Conservative Party, which was already the party of the Land and the Established Church, and which now became also the party of Big Business. The void thus created within the Liberal Party was quickly filled by a new breed of radical social reformers, such as David Lloyd George, who, whilst repudiating socialism as a doctrine, none the less advocated state action to remedy social wrongs, and the use of taxation to achieve a very modest redistribution of national resources.

This 'New Liberalism' found expression in the great reforms of the last Liberal governments (1905–15): old-age pensions; sickness and unemployment insurance; minimum wages in certain industries; free school meals for the children of the very poor. It was taken a stage further in the 'Liberal Yellow Book' of 1928 (*Britain's Industrial Future*), which was heavily influenced by Keynesian interventionism: the use of a managed economy to bring down unemployment and stimulate industrial recovery. It is worth remembering that both J.M. Keynes and Sir William Beveridge were Liberals, and that the Beveridge Reports on *Social Insurance* (1942) and *Full Employment* (1944) represented the distilled essence of what has come to be called 'Social Liberalism'. The Beveridge Reports and Keynesian economics amounted to a blueprint for the humane and efficient running of a capitalist economy; this blueprint had a major impact upon the policies of the post-war Attlee governments.

Social Liberalism triumphed; but the old Liberal Party was all but dead. Free Trade, to which the party had clung with such obsession as the Mid-Victorian Boom gave way to the Great Depression (1873–96), was finally abandoned in 1932, by which time the party's parliamentary representation had contracted to just 72 MPs, almost half of whom were allies of the National Government. In 1935 the number of Liberal MPs was reduced to 21, and in 1945 to 12; during the 1950s the figure contracted to just six, of whom five had been elected without Conservative opposition, as a result of agreements with local Conservative Parties to prevent Labour victories. Squeezed between the forces of Capital and Labour, as represented by the Conservative and Labour Parties, old Liberalism retreated into the Celtic fringes of Britain, from which much of its Nonconformist fervour had been drawn.

Just as the decline of old Liberalism had coincided with the rise of Labour in the inter-war period, so the rebirth of Liberalism took place at the same time as the electoral decline of Labour in the 1950s; but the interplay of forces was much more complex in the 1950s than in the 1920s. After the First World War a new electorate had come into being, to whom Liberalism did not appeal; in the 1950s, as the Labour Party suffered from internal doctrinal conflict and the Conservative government's handling of both domestic and foreign policy appeared weak and inept, the possibility did indeed seem to exist of enticing moderate, non-socialist Britain into the Liberal camp.

The rebirth of the Liberal Party can be precisely dated: 5 November 1956, when Jo Grimond, the MP for Orkney & Shetland, assumed the leadership of the party in succession to Clement Davies. Ever since Herbert Samuel had succeeded Lloyd George as Liberal leader (1931), Liberal strategy had been grounded in the hope that by holding the balance of power in the House of Commons it could claim a stake in a coalition government; in this way it would regain credibility and, ultimately, popularity. In 1951, when the Conservatives had been returned with a slim but viable majority (17 seats), Davies had wisely refused Churchill's offer of a ministerial post, which would probably have resulted in the complete submergence of Liberalism within the Conservative Party. In any case, the Parliament of 1951–5 was not truly 'hung'.

Grimond did not break with the idea that his party might climb back into office through a hung Parliament; but he saw that there was no immediate prospect of this taking place. Meanwhile the party needed a strategy, a framework for action that would enable it to survive and, if possible, to grow. The keys to this strategy were found within the disarray in Labour's ranks in the late 1950s, and the decline in Conservative fortunes following the Suez invasion, which was taking place at the very time of Grimond's accession to office.

At the heart of this strategy—as at the time of the establishment of the Social Democratic Party 25 years later—was the belief that the composition of the electorate was undergoing fundamental change of the sort that would make it respond positively to new ideas. Grimond read the message of the Labour defeat of 1955, and of the consequent research into Labour's declining popularity, and he knew that public opinion had turned against further nationalisation and further state involvement in people's lives. But whereas Gaitskell's prescription (based on this diagnosis) was to try and make the Labour Party less unlike the Conservatives, Grimond's answer was to differentiate much more sharply Liberalism from Conservatism, and he chose to do this by resurrecting Social Liberalism in a new guise, namely that of an appeal to progressive forces, anxious for further domestic reform but hostile to the class rhetoric of the Labour Party and to its close relationship with trade unions.

Under Grimond the party was quite unambiguously relocated on the centre-left of the political spectrum: it opposed the Suez adventure, Britain's independent nuclear deterrent, and the retention of all land bases (except Singapore) east of Suez, but it also expressed reservations about the power of trade unions, favoured European integration, home-ownership and tax cuts, and professed to be gravely agitated by the question of individual freedom. In the three general elections which the party fought under Grimond's leadership this amalgam appeared to strike a chord with the voters. The number of Liberal MPs grew from six (1959) to 12 (1966); between 1959 and 1963 party membership doubled to well over 300,000; the party appeared able to hold its own against both Labour and Conservative opposition (as evidenced by Eric Lubbock's spectacular by-election success at Orpington in March 1962); and in the early 1960s it notched up an impressive list of local-election successes, particularly in urban districts, a few of which fell briefly under Liberal control.

This rapid improvement in party fortunes was followed by an even more rapid fall. In 1966 half the Parliamentary Liberal Party came from English seats. But in 1970 the total fell once more to six, four of whom represented Scottish and Welsh constituencies. In popular terms the party continued to do relatively well, as Table 3.1 indicates; its under-representation in the Commons was a gross injustice, against which it had every right to complain. Yet even as we acknowledge that its popular appeal had grown, we must also recognise that this appeal remained limited.

Table 3.2 gives the proportions of the socio-economic groups AB, C1, C2 and DE voting Liberal at general elections between 1964 and 1974. The basis of the Grimond revival had been the unpopularity

Table 3.1 The Liberal vote, 1955–1979

	Total vote		% vote per opposed candidate	MPs elected
1955	722,405	(2.7%)	15.1	6
1959	1,638,571	(5.9%)	16.9	6
1964	3,092,878	(11.2%)	18.5	9
1966	2,327,535	(8.5%)	16.1	12
1970	2,117,033	(7.5%)	13.5	6
1974 (F)	6,063,470	(19.3%)	23.6	14
1974 (O)	5,346,754	(18.3%)	18.9	13
1979	4,313,811	(13.8%)	14.9	11

Table 3.2 Liberal voting by occupational class, 1964–1974

	AB	C1	C2	DE
1964	15	14	11	9
1966	11	11	8	7
1970	10	9	7	6
1974 (F)	20	25	20	17
1974 (O)	22	21	20	16

Source: NOP data as reproduced in Nuffield election studies.

of the Conservative government, coupled with the disarray in the ranks of Labour. But the argument advanced by Liberals to support the contention that 'their time had come' was rather different: namely, that a new salaried professional class had already emerged, while the working class had fragmented under the pressures created by affluence. Processes which were indeed under way (though in a far more complex manner, and over a far lengthier time-span) were deemed to be largely complete. This explanation was, however, rooted more deeply in myth than in reality. There could be no question of the Liberal Party challenging the Conservatives as the party of the right; some disenchanted Conservative supporters were clearly attracted to Liberalism, but only by way of protest and to keep Labour out.

Equally, however, as a party of the left, the Liberal appeal fell flat; as Table. 3.2 shows, manual-worker support for the party actually contracted between 1964 and 1970. Liberalism was conspicuous by its inability to make much headway in capturing urban seats held by Labour. Colne Valley, won from Labour in 1966, and Birmingham Ladywood, captured in 1969, were both lost at the 1970 general election, when Orpington once more elected a Conservative MP. Once support for Labour began to revive between 1962 and 1964, hopes of a genuine, radical readjustment of the political system quickly faded.

There was a pathetic epilogue to this story. Labour's overall majority of four seats following the 1964 election led to a great deal of public discussion of a Lib-Lab pact; the speculation was intensified following Labour's loss of the Leyton seat to the Conservatives in January 1965, and of the Roxburgh seat to the Liberal David Steel two months later. Grimond began to talk as a partner in a coalition government, offering support in the division lobbies in return for an agreed radical programme. But, sensing that the tide was running strongly in *his* favour, Harold Wilson politely rebuffed these advances, but took care to offer Roderick Bowen, Liberal MP for Cardiganshire, the post of Deputy-Chairman of Ways and Means. Bowen—in effect—defected, and Labour's immediate crisis was solved. Grimond waited until after the 1966 election, which gave Labour a secure majority, and then resigned as Liberal leader.

The period of office of his successor, the extrovert television personality Jeremy Thorpe (leader 1967–76), coincided with a phase of British electoral development which was, as we have seen, genuinely more fluid and, on the face of it, more receptive to ideas of moderate radicalism. Until the election of February 1974 the Liberals were in no position to pose as a parliamentary 'third force'; indeed the contest of 1970 cut the number of Liberal MPs by a half. Under Thorpe the party became a haven for the discontented and the frustrated—those who were alienated by Labour's failure to live up to its socialist promise, or whose particular concerns could not be accommodated within two-party politics.

This development proved a source of great strength but also of great weakness. Under the umbrella of the Young Liberals a motley collection of pressure groups, concerned with matters as diverse as apartheid in South Africa and housing in Britain's inner cities, proclaimed themselves to be true adherents of the Liberal tradition. By opposing the Kenyan Asians Exclusion Act passed by the Labour government in 1968, the Parliamentary Liberal Party reinforced this new image of a Liberalism more radical than Labourism; David Steel's successful private members' bill to reform the abortion laws gave the image further tangible credibility.

The exploitation of 'community politics' was also encouraging. Shorn of its theoretical pretensions, community politics meant nothing more than the exploitation of local issues for national political purposes. Sensing—correctly—that many citizens felt frustrated by their seeming inability to influence and control the immediate environment in which they lived, Liberals offered themselves as unpaid organisers of prefabricated pressure groups, complete with newsletters and advice centres, to which those who felt helpless could turn. Community politics meant anything and everything, from campaigning to have a bus-stop moved or broken paving-stones replaced to organising against faceless vested interests involved in controversial planning appeals and housing schemes. In this way Liberal activists became known, and were able to capitalise on this support at local-authority level. By 1973 the Liberals had become the largest party on Liverpool City Council, and had made advances in centres as far apart as Eastbourne, Pendle, Birmingham, Sheffield, Leeds and parts of London.

Community politics not only paid handsome electoral dividends. It offered many Liberals their first taste of power (albeit in a local context), gave the party a high media profile and, partly as a result, accelerated the much-needed membership drive. A string of parliamentary by-election successes seemed to confirm the benefits of this strategy: Birmingham Ladywood (1969); Rochdale and Sutton & Cheam (1972); the Isle of Ely, Ripon and Berwick (1973). Indeed, the Liberal revival of 1972–4, culminating in the return to Westminster of 14 Liberal MPs in February 1974, representing 19.3 per cent of the total UK vote, appeared at the time as a dramatic vindication of the community strategy, which had been endorsed, at the behest of the Young Liberals, at the 1970 Liberal Assembly. Never before had over six million electors voted Liberal in the polling booths.

Spectacular though this period was for Liberal fortunes, it turned out to be a dawn which was not merely false, but dangerously so. To begin with, there were aspects of community politics, of concern with environmental and ecological issues, of over-zealous and occasionally intolerant militancy, that gave the party an almost Maoist image; the Young Liberals replaced the Young Communists as the collective voice of angry and impatient youth, but their antics (for example their involvement in disrupting sporting fixtures involving visiting teams from South Africa) alienated those disgruntled Conservatives who needed to be won over for Liberalism. In any case, many voters wondered how such tactics could be squared with a 'Liberal' outlook.

Community politics could of course be slotted without difficulty into a Liberal philosophy, in the important sense of a concern to emphasise the autonomy of local communities at the expense of the apparatus of central government. But the implication that could be read into the community strategy, of a return to the individualist approach, worried those whose commitment to Social Liberalism was still strong. There was something almost anarchistic in community politics: liberate people from 'the centre' and they will be truly free; but would this necessarily result in a greater measure of social justice on a national scale?

Most serious of all was the effect which the embrace of community politics had upon the development of an overall Liberal policy. In the eyes of the electorate community politics was an approach, a tactic, a device and—in some quarters—a gimmick; it was never looked upon as an ideology, something by which Liberalism could be distinguished from Labourism, Socialism and Conservatism. The hypnotic effect of community politics, symbolised by the blossoming of the Association of Liberal Councillors, diverted the party itself from the need to develop a coherent and distinctive programme. Home Rule for Scotland and Wales, which was the most original feature of the 1970 Liberal manifesto, was hardly calculated to spearhead a national revival of party fortunes.

So the failure of the Liberals to benefit from the decline in Labour's popularity in 1970 was hardly surprising. The revival experienced during the Heath government was based on local issues, flamboyant personalities such as Cyril Smith (Rochdale) and Clement Freud (Isle of Ely), and the general unpopularity of the Conservatives; it did not arise from any novel policy initiatives. At the election of February 1974 the Liberals produced little that had not been said before or which was not being said by the Conservatives or Labour: statutory controls on prices and wages; repeal of the 1971 Industrial Relations Act and of the 1972 Housing Finance Act (which had attempted to reduce the rate-subsidy of rents for local-authority housing); reform of the EEC; taxation of oil-company profits; the well-worn theme of decentralisation. For the October 1974 election the Liberals did not even bother to produce a new manifesto. Instead they offered the electors a 16-page summary of what had been said eight months previously.

In 1970 the Liberal Party figured very much as a fringe group in media presentation of the election. But in February 1974 the party became the centre of intense interest, because evidence emerged of an upsurge in Liberal support, at the expense of the Conservatives, as the campaign neared its conclusion. On 1 March 1974 Jeremy Thorpe found himself the leader of a group of MPs whose support was being actively pursued by Edward Heath in a desperate bid to cling to office. The Liberals were offered the chance of participating in a Coalition, with a Cabinet seat for Thorpe; in return Heath held out the promise of a Speaker's Conference on electoral reform. Thorpe consulted his parliamentary colleagues, who were united in rejecting the offer, though they held out the possibility of Liberal participation in a government of national unity. Heath resigned to make way for a minority Labour administration.

In the immediate aftermath of the election it seemed that the Liberals had been right to reject Heath's offer. Although Liberal candidates seem to have attracted support evenly from both major parties, most of their victories and almost all of their near-misses had resulted from the anti-Conservative mood. Moreover, a Conservative-Liberal coalition would still have been eight votes short of a parliamentary majority: the Liberals would have shared office but not power, and would have been blamed for having sustained a government that was reckoned to be deeply unpopular.

With the passage of years, however, and the admitted advantage of hindsight, the wisdom of the Liberal parliamentarians—in taking a decision which, it must be said, reflected widespread grassroots feeling—can be questioned. The excellent Liberal vote in February had been based upon the unpopularity of other parties. It was not a vote for Liberalism, an unpalatable fact that was, however, supported by opinion poll evidence showing (for example) that most Liberal voters were hostile towards the Common Market. The 14 Liberal MPs could make little impact at Westminster, and began to be more receptive to the idea of coalition, preferably with Labour. During the summer of 1974 deep divisions emerged within the party on the whole issue of participation in a coalition government. On 29 June the party's National Executive Committee came out against coalition with either the Labour Party or the Conservatives. But Thorpe, and his Chief Whip, David Steel, continued to talk of participation in a national government committed to an agreed programme to solve the country's economic problems.

The electorate was understandably bewildered. In the constituencies Liberals acted as if the party might form a government by itself whenever the next election was called. There was a rushed effort to organise the Liberal vote in Labour-held seats, so raising the total number of seats contested in October to an unprecedented 619 and placing additional burdens on party resources and party funds. The party ought to have concentrated on exploiting its strength in the Conservative marginals; instead the militant radicalism of its activists frightened would-be Tory defectors. Because it had refused to join a Coalition with the Conservatives, it was accused of having willed a Labour government into being. Because it had refused, subsequently, to join a Coalition with Labour it was accused of having aided and abetted weak minority government. The call for a government of national unity was frankly incredible and absurd—the day-dream, perhaps, of a party that had backed away from the responsibilities of office and which might not be worthy of or capable of undertaking them.

At the October 1974 election the party suffered for its indecisiveness; younger voters seem to have deserted to Labour, while in suburban areas about ten seats that Labour might have won were retained by the Conservatives due to Liberal defections, especially among older voters. In consequence the Liberal vote fell and it emerged with fewer MPs than the Welsh and Scottish Nationalists combined. Its policies seem to have been misunderstood—or simply not understood at all—by the electorate, who found difficulty placing it anywhere on the political spectrum.

Between October 1974 and May 1979 the nationwide standing of the Liberal Party drifted downwards almost without respite. In October 1974 the Liberals, though they had squandered their opportunity to make an electoral breakthrough, still attracted the support of almost 19 per cent of the voters; two years later the standing of the party had fallen by a half, and by the early months of 1979 it was barely above 5 per cent. Of the 29 by-elections that took place during the Parliament of 1974–9 the Liberal vote fell in all but two (Newcastle Central, October 1976 and the victory at Liverpool Edge Hill, March 1979). Taking all these by-election contests together, the Liberals averaged 12.4 per cent of the votes, and in the circumstances they did well to attract nearly 15 per cent at the 1979 election. None the less, the number of Liberal MPs fell again in 1979, when the party found itself once more consigned to political impotence.

The central features of Liberal history in this period of near-minority and (from June 1975) virtual minority government were the personal misfortunes of Jeremy Thorpe and the boyish enthusiasm of David Steel, his successor as party Leader. A Department of Trade report on London & Counties Securities, of which Thorpe had been a director, raised issues of company malpractice which inevitably reflected upon Thorpe's own conduct. At the same time (January 1976) rumours which had been current for some time concerning Thorpe's alleged homosexuality were given new credence through statements made in court by Norman Scott, a male model. These events culminated in August 1978 when Thorpe and others were charged with conspiring to murder Scott; on 22 June 1979 all, including Thorpe, were acquitted. By then Thorpe no longer led the party. He resigned the leadership on 10 May 1976, but continued as an MP and, indeed, defended his seat at Devon North in 1979, losing it to the Conservatives.

The Thorpe affair reacted badly upon the public image of the Liberal Party, whose parliamentary representatives were perceived as having chosen and tolerated a man of whom it might fairly be said that he had put his own personal interests above those of his party. The election of David Steel (12 June 1976), by a new method in which all party members participated did nothing to restore party fortunes. John Pardoe, Steel's opponent, was a convert from Labour, a radical whose tough, tub-thumping style delighted many constituency activists but frightened those whose vision of the Liberal future was moderate and moderating. Steel was a radical, too, but he was a man of quiet diplomacy and, within limits, a realist. That is to say, he doubted the long-term wisdom of the community approach, appreciating that it could repel as well as attract, and he wondered whether, given the vagaries of the first-past-the-post electoral system, the Liberals were capable of making a parliamentary impact even if (as in February 1974) millions voted for them.

Under Steel electoral reform remained, of course, an ultimate Liberal hope. In a system of proportional representation Liberals would have to show a willingness to enter into negotiations with other parties to form and sustain a government. In his speech to the Liberal Assembly at Llandudno in 1976 Steel made it clear that he would be prepared to enter into a coalition or some other co-operative arrangement even before electoral reform had been achieved and without waiting for some dramatic realignment of the electorate in the Liberals' favour. The opportunity to put this policy to the test came in March 1977, but in circumstances that predestined it to failure.

The Lib-Lab pact of 1977–8 arose from Jim Callaghan's desire to remain in office despite abundant signs that his government was deeply unpopular, and from the desire of the Parliamentary Liberal Party to smell and taste 'power', even if they could not actually possess it. Liberal MPs had opposed much of Labour's legislative programme, especially those measures giving additional rights and freedoms to the trade-union movement. They were rightly suspicious of Labour's attitude towards the Common Market; but they applauded the decision to hold a referendum on this issue (5 June 1975) and its outcome—an overwhelming 'Yes' vote—was held up as a vindication of Liberal policy. Direct elections to the European Parliament and the establishment of devolved government in Scotland and Wales could also be slotted into the main-frame of Liberal ideals, with the added attraction of the possibility of proportional representation in each case. Agreement on direct elections and devolution, with free votes on proportional representation, were major features of the pact. The Liberal Party (in effect, the Parliamentary Liberal Party) was to be consulted on government policy; major disagreements were to be ironed out personally by Callaghan and Steel. In return, Liberal MPs agreed to support the Labour government on votes of confidence in the Commons.

From the Liberal point of view the pact was a bad deal, which became worse as time progressed. The Labour government gave away nothing in agreeing to it; on the contrary, Labour was sustained in office for over a year, merely by consenting to consult Liberal MPs. On a few issues of tertiary importance Labour gave ground, and the government had to bow to Liberal pressure to forgo an increase in petrol duty. In July 1977 Liberal MPs agreed to renew the pact for another year, brushing aside the evidence of extreme annoyance within Liberal constituency parties, based upon the undoubted fact that the agreement, far from boosting party popularity (which had exhibited a modest rise during the second half of 1976) had allowed it to fall to its lowest level since 1974.

On 14 December 1977 less than half the Labour MPs voted for the regional list system of proportional representation for direct elections to the European Parliament; in consequence the proposal, which had been a central feature of the Lib-Lab pact, was defeated. The following day, more out of loyalty to David Steel than out of love for the pact, Liberal MPs voted by 6 to 4 in favour of its continuation, which now depended on Labour agreement either to proportional representation for the Scottish Assembly or to a referendum on proportional representation at Westminster. There was not the remotest chance of either proposal being accepted. In May 1978 Steel gave notice that the pact would not be renewed after the summer recess, apparently believing that Callaghan would be obliged to call a general election later that year. This did not happen. Sensing a revival in Labour support, as reflected in opinion polls and by-elections, Callaghan postponed an election contest until the following year, when the Liberal vote was further squeezed and the number of Liberal MPs fell to eleven.

David Steel argued that the pact had been a success, because it had ensured some measure of political stability and moderated Labour policies. The moderating influence of the pact seems hard to accept, since the Labour left was in no position to force its policies upon the Labour government, let alone the House of Commons. Even if we agree that the pact ensured stability, this was not how it was perceived in the eyes of the voting public, who did not thank the Liberal Party for having entered into it. It seems probable that many who had voted Liberal in the boom year of 1974 turned or returned to the Tories five years later out of disgust that the Liberals had kept Labour in office. The pact may well have been a noble gesture: noble gestures are not what politics is all about.

On the morrow of the 1979 election the bankruptcy of Liberal strategy over the past quarter-century was crystal clear. A majority of Liberal MPs (seven out of eleven) now sat for English constituencies. Three of the seats held by the Liberals at that election were in the industrial north of England (Liverpool Edge Hill, Rochdale and Colne Valley), where Labour posed the major challenge. Elsewhere, however, the Conservatives were the greater threat, and the ten seats which the Liberals came closest to winning in 1979 were all won by Conservative candidates. The contradictory claims of those Liberals who urged an appeal to disillusioned Conservatives and those who wished to exploit divisions in the Labour Party seemed irreconcilable. The attempt to act as a third force in Parliament had not been a success. Community politics brought support but also created problems. Above all, the party had no distinctive ideology. The major features of its 1979 manifesto (electoral reform; a federal Britain; and a Bill of Rights) aroused little popular enthusiasm. The party had spent over half a century in the political wilderness without reaching the promised land or even knowing in which direction it was to be found.

We noted earlier in this chapter how remarkably even support for Liberalism was among different occupational groups. In 1979 MORI found that within a combined A, B and C1 category Liberal support had stood at 16 per cent, within C2 at 15 per cent, and within D and E at 13 per cent. This truly 'classless' appeal was paraded as a source of strength. In fact it was a source—perhaps the major source—of Liberal weakness. Liberalism no longer had a geographical base; nor was it rooted in a sectional appeal that might have provided it with core support, dependable and economically cohesive. The evidence of attitude surveys suggests that the only beliefs held in common among Liberal *voters* (as distinct from party members) were an aversion to further nationalisation and a preference for the maintenance of government services rather than cuts in taxation.

The 1979 manifesto reflected these views, but the fall in the Liberal vote—like the upsurge in support five years previously—lends credence to the view that, at any rate during the 1970s, only about 10 per cent of the electorate regarded voting Liberal as anything more than a form of protest, like not voting at all. The party identification of Liberal voters was weak, and the support overall was fickle in the extreme. During the 1970s the Conservative and Labour Parties could rely on a quarter of the electorate remaining loyal between one election and the next; for the Liberal Party the figure was a worthless 2 per cent. Many voters evinced a sympathy with the party, and said they might have voted Liberal had it had a chance of forming a government. Since it evidently did not, expressions of sympathy were not translated into solid attachment. In any case, under the first-past-the-post system a party needs to win at least 30 per cent of the votes to be rewarded with a respectable number of Commons' seats; the post-war Liberal Party was incapable of jumping this hurdle.

Thus, whatever realignments and dealignments were experienced by the electorate in the 1970s, the Liberal Party lost out. That it did not die out was due entirely to the convulsions that engulfed Labour after its 1979 defeat, and which culminated in the formation of the breakaway Social Democratic Party.

The SDP was founded by a group of anti-socialist Labour politicians who took fright at the penetration of the Labour Party by the hard left in the 1970s. In the history of Labour there had been moments when a split of this type had seemed imminent, especially during Gaitskell's period as Leader. Arguably Gaitskell's greatest contribution to Labour's well-being was to have died when he did; Harold Wilson's management technique papered over the cracks, enabling the coalition of socialists and social democrats to survive into the 1970s. But the coalition could not outlive attempts to re-write the terms under which it had functioned hitherto.

The SDP was formally launched on 26 March 1981. Its prospectus—the Limehouse Declaration issued by Roy Jenkins, David Owen, Bill Rodgers and Shirley Williams—had been published on 25 January. Owen, Rodgers and Williams had already (7 June 1980) declared that they would leave the Labour Party if it committed itself to withdrawal from the Common Market, which the party Conference did the following October, when it also endorsed unilateral nuclear disarmament. Meanwhile, the Labour Party's NEC had signalled its intention of proposing an electoral college for the election of the Labour Leader; this also, as we have seen, was endorsed by Conference in October. The choice of Michael Foot to succeed Jim Callaghan (10 November) was a reflection of the extent to which the balance of power even within the Parliamentary Labour Party was swinging rapidly in a socialist direction.

The endorsement of the electoral college at the special Wembley Conference the following January with 40 per cent of the electoral-college votes going to the trade unions, and the imposition of mandatory reselection of Labour MPs tipped the balance of opinion in favour of a breakaway party. The promulgation of the Limehouse Declaration was accompanied by the launch of the Council for Social Democracy (CSD), which almost at once welcomed into membership nine Labour MPs (Tom Bradley, Richard Crawshaw, Tom Ellis, John Horam, Robert Maclennan, John Roper, Neville Sandelson, Mike Thomas and Ian Wrigglesworth) and a significant number of local Labour councillors. On 5 February *The Guardian* carried a 'Declaration' of support for the Council from an array of show-business personalities, entrepreneurs, sportsmen and women and moderate trade unionists (pre-eminently Frank Chapple, of the electricians). By the time of the SDP's formal establishment it could boast the adhesion of a number of peers (including nine who had hitherto taken the Labour whip) and a Conservative defector, the MP Christopher Brocklebank-Fowler.

Several quite distinct sets of considerations operated in the minds of those who created this new political animal. At one level there was profound disagreement with aspects of Labour policy, notably unilateralism and withdrawal from the EEC. Roy Jenkins had resigned as Deputy Leader of the Labour Party in 1971, following the party's call for a referendum on EEC membership. Five years later, after Callaghan had refused to appoint him as Foreign Secretary, Jenkins had accepted the post of President of the European Commission in Brussels. Labour's attitude to the EEC, and the implications for British membership of NATO of the adoption of unilateralism, seemed (in the words of the Limehouse Declaration) to be 'isolationist, xenophobic or neutralist', a recipe for British impotence in the counsels of the nations.

At another level, the founders of the SDP rejected the moves then current to widen participation in the election of the Labour Leader, and to make Labour MPs more accountable to the local parties who selected them and who worked for their election to the House of Commons. Social Democracy was, in this sense, profoundly and unashamedly anti-democratic and elitist. 'The calamitous outcome of the Labour Party Wembley Conference [the Limehouse Declaration extolled] demands a new start in British politics. A handful of trade union leaders can now dictate the choice of a future Prime Minister. The conference disaster is the culmination of a long process by which the [Labour] party has moved steadily away from its roots in the people of this country and its commitment to parliamentary government.' Accordingly, the constitution of the SDP provided for Area (rather than Constituency) Parties, which would be less susceptible to control by small groups of activists, and for policy-formulation to remain clearly within the remit of SDP MPs; the SDP Assembly could make its views known, but could not tell MPs what to do in Parliament.

Did the founders of the SDP really envisage its having a secure future as a separate party, ready to co-operate with other parties but maintaining its own independence? Of did they harbour the thought that its establishment would precipitate a break-up of the Labour Party and a fundamental realignment at the top of British politics, resulting in the ultimate fusion of Liberals with Social Democrats to form a new party capable of replacing Labour and winning power for itself? Many of the troubles that subsequently befell the SDP resulted from failure explicitly to address these questions at the outset.

In his Dimbleby lecture (22 November 1979) Roy Jenkins had called for proportional representation and for a 'strengthening of the radical centre'. But it was clear that PR could only come as a result of a fundamental realignment: neither Labour nor the Conservatives were going to enact PR, unless forced to do so by a substantial third force in the Commons; even then, there was (and is) every chance of an unholy alliance of Conservative and Labour

MPs to defeat it. If the first-past-the-post system had worked unfairly against the Liberals, how much more so would it work against a fourth party, the Social Democrats? Jenkins and his supporters knew this very well. Hence their preference for a merger with the Liberals, perhaps made easier and more palatable by a process of ever-closer co-operation with them. Meanwhile, defections from Labour were to be encouraged. Foot's election as Labour Leader had been made possible partly because a number of future members of the SDP had mischievously voted for him. We can therefore treat with a large pinch of salt the outrage expressed at Limehouse with the results of the Wembley Conference. SDP supporters were openly delighted as the process of mandatory reselection got under way, and brought more Labour refugees into their camp.

But there were those—pre-eminently David Owen—who took the view that what was being constructed was a genuine, free-standing left-of-centre party in its own right, a sort of Gaitskellite Labour Party, freed from the intolerant militancy of the hard left, radical less in its vision of a socialist society (though Owen liked to describe himself still as a 'socialist') than in its opposition to the seeming determination of Thatcherite Conservatism to dismantle all the good that had come out of Labour administrations. Of the Gang of Four that issued the Limehouse Declaration, Owen had been the most difficult to convince of the necessity of leaving the Labour Party; he became the most determined of the Four to remain loyal to the new party he had helped construct.

Did this new party have a constituency to whom it could legitimately appeal? The SDP, as befits a child of its time, had been thoroughly market-researched. On 10 December 1980 two of the country's leading electoral sociologists, Ivor Crewe and Anthony King, had attended a meeting at Shirley Williams' London flat; also present at the meeting were John Horam, Robert Maclennan, Bill Rodgers, John Roper, Mike Thomas and Ian Wrigglesworth. Crewe and King are both Professors in Essex University's Department of Government, from which the British Election Study had been conducted. The findings of this study had hitherto been confined to the pages of learned journals and specialist conferences. Crewe, Co-Director of the Study, argued that the corrosive effect of partisan dealignment on both the Conservative and (especially) the Labour vote had resulted in a less committed, more volatile electorate that might welcome the chance to support a new centre party.

At the time the virtues of purely statistical analysis seemed compelling. When a by-election occurred at Warrington (16 July 1981) Roy Jenkins, standing for the SDP with Liberal support, obtained 42.4 per cent of the votes (the previous Liberal performance had been 9.0 per cent), and came within 1,800 votes of winning the seat; a constituency that had been considered rock-solid Labour in 1979 had now become a marginal. The theorists of Essex seemed to have been vindicated.

The enormous publicity generated by the arrival of the SDP had brought its own success. Some Liberals, such as Cyril Smith, were sceptical of the long-term future of the SDP as a fourth party. Others (with the notable exception of David Owen) urged a formal arrangement that would go well beyond mere electoral pacts. In June the two parties produced a joint policy state-ment, *A Fresh Start For Britain*, and in September the Liberals, meeting at Llandudno, endorsed the Alliance, which was to involve the presentation of a common manifesto and the imple-mentation of electoral pacts nationwide in time for the next general election.

The story of the Alliance (1981–8) is a story of glorious failure. For most Liberals it represented a new way forward, an escape from depressing and apparently endless stagnation, a chance to occupy at last the centre of the political stage. The Alliance was not a marriage of equals. The SDP had twice as many MPs as the Liberals, and included amongst these was, without question, a glittering array of forceful and brilliant politicians, some of whom, like Owen and Williams, had held Cabinet office. Jenkins re-entered Parliament as MP for Glasgow Hillhead in March 1982 and became, in fact if not in name, the Prime Minister Designate of a future Alliance government. Owen, a former Foreign Secretary (and the youngest holder of that office since William Pitt) enjoyed an international reputation. His firm anti-unilateralist views were bound to cause friction with radical Liberals, but for the moment both partners to the Alliance basked in his reflected glory, which he obviously enjoyed.

The immediate popularity of the Alliance had been established at Warrington, and it was confirmed at North-West Croydon (October 1981), which was won by the Liberal Bill Pitt, Crosby (November), which returned Shirley Williams to the Commons, and Roy Jenkins' victory in Glasgow. All these successes were achieved at the expense of the Tories, whose share of the vote fell by an average of 16.8 per cent. The Alliance's impact on Labour-held seats was less impressive. The first such by-election, at Mitcham on 3 June 1982, saw a very gratifying rise in the Alliance vote (+ 20.5 per cent), but this was not quite enough to prevent a Conservative victory; Labour retained Coatbridge (24 June), Gower (16 September), Peckham (28 October), Glasgow Queen's Park (2 December) and Darlington (24 March 1983). The Alliance did register one spectacular success in a Labour seat, when they romped home at Bermondsey (24 February 1983) with almost 58 per cent of the votes. But the Bermondsey Labour Party was split, the 'official' Labour candidate, Peter Tatchell, having been disowned by the NEC because of his favourable view of extra-parliamentary action.

In short, although the electoral future of the Alliance was said to be bound up with the fate of an ailing Labour Party, the actual gains being registered appeared to have resulted from the votes of disenchanted Conservatives. This paradox haunted the Alliance, and the contradictions from which it stemmed were never properly resolved. On the Liberal side of the Alliance, almost half the 1983 Liberal vote came from former Liberal supporters; defections from Conservative and Labour to Liberal were of the same order of magnitude. But over 40 per cent of SDP support was derived from former Labour voters; the aggregate of defections from Conservative to SDP was only about half this size.[1] Taking the Alliance vote as a whole, in 1983 (see Table 1:9) 13 per cent of 1979 Tory voters defected to it, compared with 22 per cent of those who had in 1979 voted Labour; the Alliance, in turn, lost only 9 per cent of its support *to* Labour, but 14 per cent to the Conservatives.

The Liberal Party had fed off the Tories; the SDP fed off the Labour Party; and the marriage of the two had produced a coalition that seemed destined to do better in an anti-Labour than in an anti-Conservative guise. But political reality is seldom so logical. In the race for office it is seats that count, not votes. Just as important, nowadays, is the fact that, except for nationalist parties, campaigning is a countrywide event, not something that can be confined to individual constituencies and varied to suit the particular needs of each. In 1983 Alliance strategists noted that of the 80 seats that were reckoned to be most *winnable*, no less than 78 were Tory held.

In the early 1980s, prior to the 1983 general election, Alliance publicists painted a very rosy picture of its future. Some opinion polls gave it as much as 50 per cent of the vote, and though wiser counsels might have pointed out that a party, or coalition, whose support is susceptible to wild fluctuations (from 50 per cent to 20 per cent according to the polls, and from 57.7 per cent (Bermondsey) to 8.2 per cent (Coatbridge) according to by-election results) must be presumed not to have deep foundations, the euphoria of the moment carried all before it. One writer, in 1982, admitted that the Alliance could 'still suffer setbacks', but remained adamant that 'whatever Labour and Tories do . . . would seem unlikely to change *the political trend* favouring the Alliance', which he declared 'should win' the next general election.[2]

There was, of course, no such trend, merely a mid-term mood that could easily be blown away as an election approached, and voters had to choose a government rather than merely register a protest. On this electoral battlefield the Alliance was obliged to face both ways and, as with the Liberals a decade earlier, the remarkable evenness of its class support (see Table 3.3) proved a devastating handicap.

Table 3.3 Alliance voting by occupational class (%), 1983 and 1987

	ABC1	C2DE
1983	28	22
1987	26	21

Source: as for Table 1.3.

Without proportional representation, and in a situation in which Conservative and Labour (especially Labour) support was becoming more geographically located, across-the-board appeal may lead to more votes (as it clearly did in 1983), but is unlikely to produce many, or any, more seats. There was very little likelihood of the Alliance making significant headway in Labour strongholds; worse still, a nationwide swing to the Alliance, resulting, perhaps, in the capture of Tory marginals, could only improve Labour's chances of forming a government.

The difficulties that these facts of political life posed for Alliance constituency tactics also spilled over into its programme strategy. In 1982–3 the hammering out of a common set of policies did not prove difficult, but the two major disagreements, over statutory control of trade unions and nuclear defence, were straws in the wind. As we have seen, an element in the SDP revolt against Labour had been alarm at the power of trade unions. The SDP preferred statutory control of union activities, including compulsory ballots before strike actions; the Liberals acquiesced in this proposal, though they remained adamant that such control was impractical. More seriously, the two parties could not agree over defence policy. Again, the origin of this dispute is to be found in the events that had led to the SDP-Labour schism. David Owen had sensed that the unilateralism of the Labour Party was a vote-loser, but he was unable to persuade the Liberals that opposition to the siting of Cruise missiles in Britain (a policy that most Liberals espoused) would, equally, repel rather than attract. The two sides agreed to differ.

The 1983 Alliance manifesto reflected the preponderating influence that SDP leaders had had in its drafting. In 1979 the Liberals had made electoral reform their 'first priority', and had given it pride of place in their manifesto; in 1983 proportional representation, though declared 'the linchpin of our entire programme of radical reform', appeared half-way through the manifesto document, after economic, industrial and social policy.

The lead item in 1983 was the commitment to reduce unemployment by over one million in two years, through a massive injection of taxpayers' money into the economy, and to reduce taxes only where such a reduction (for example, abolition of the National Insurance Surcharge) was likely to have a direct and immediate impact on jobs and prices. An Alliance government would establish, in consultation with unions and management, an annual range for pay settlements in the private sector, and would set up an independent Assessment Board for public service pay. Although a 'fully statutory incomes policy' was not ruled out, there was to be legislation to institute a Counter Inflation Tax, levied on companies paying above the agreed range. Unions were to be subject to compulsory secret ballots for the election of their national executives and (where 10 per cent of the membership demanded it) before the calling of an official strike. Privatisation of publicly owned industries was ruled out, but so was further nationalisation. And, in deference to Liberal die-hards, proposals were also included aimed at creating devolved assemblies in Scotland, Wales and the English regions.

These proposals turned out to be radical enough to attract almost a quarter of Labour's 1979 vote; the Alliance alone registered an increase in support in 1983, with 7.8 million electors voting for it. In Great Britain as a whole the Alliance polled 26.1 per cent of the votes, but returned only 23 MPs—less than 4 per cent of the House of Commons: a gross and inexcusable disproportion, for which the Alliance itself cannot be blamed. Yet according to the BBC Gallup survey a full quarter of the entire electorate had *considered* voting Alliance, but had not actually done so. Some Alliance victories were due in large measure to personal appeal (David Owen at Devonport, for example, and Robert Maclennan at Caithness). Others, particularly on the Liberal side, seem to have resulted from substantial tactical votes aimed at preventing Labour victories: for example, Paddy Ashdown's win at Yeovil, where the Labour vote dropped by over 16 per cent.

The Alliance had indeed succeeded in attracting support, and in that sense it—rather than the SDP alone—had broken the mould of English (but not Scottish or Welsh) politics. But the picture which the electorate had of it lacked crispness and definition; although it gained over a quarter of the votes, only about 16 per cent of voters strongly identified with it. Most British voters have no recent experience of voting for coalitions, and certainly none of voting for coalitions with two leaders. The division of seats between Liberal and SDP candidates had, in the circumstances, gone surprisingly well. But Liberal activists had not taken kindly to the intervention of SDP carpet-baggers, and many found it uncomfortable (to say the least) to support candidates, such as Shirley Williams, whose policies as members of the Labour governments of the 1970s they had strenuously opposed. In three constituencies (Hackney South, Hammersmith and Liverpool Broadgreen) local differences had not been resolved by polling day, so that official Liberal and SDP candidates opposed each other as well as the nominees of the Labour and Conservative Parties.

Above all, the results of the 1983 election demonstrated that in a genuine three-party system difficulties of the most acute kind lay in the way of an Alliance 'breakthrough' at parliamentary level. The Alliance was seen, inevitably, as an anti-Conservative party; but it was difficult to meet the criticism that its intervention had given Mrs Thatcher another four or five years of power. After 1983, given the internal warfare that raged within the Labour movement, Alliance leaders ought to have given overriding consideration to the task of hastening the destruction of the Labour Party, for which they could then offer themselves as a radical but definitely non-socialist alternative. However, the Alliance failed to meet this challenge.

Again, the evidence of by-election results after 1983 was deceptive. The performance of the Alliance in the 16 mainland by-election contests that separated the general elections of 1983 and 1987 was, on the face of it, outstanding. In only one case did its share of the vote decline (Cynon Valley, May 1984). Overall its average share was 34.6 per cent, and in three instances (Ryedale, May 1986; Greenwich, February 1987; and Truro, March 1987) its share was over 50 per cent. These successes were achieved not merely in the South and the South-West of England, but also in northern Labour strongholds, such as Chesterfield and Tyne Bridge. Levels of support such as these were taken as strong circumstantial evidence that the one-third breakthrough had been achieved: that is, that the Alliance was at last capable of attracting support large enough for it to be rewarded with a significant share of the representation at Westminster.

We know that this was not to be. Of the four by-election gains registered by the Alliance, only one was at the expense of Labour, namely Rosie Barnes' win at Greenwich, where the Labour Party was split into hard-left and not-so-hard-left factions. The remaining three (Portsmouth South, Brecon and Ryedale) were at the expense of the Conservatives, and of these the first and the last were won back by the Tories in June 1987. When the 1987 election was announced, opinion polls gave the Alliance just 25 per cent of the votes—less than half the proportions registered at Greenwich and Truro a few months before—and this percentage actually drifted downwards during the campaign; on polling day the support turned out to be just 22.6 per cent, lower (that is) than in 1983.

Some beliefs dearly held by Alliance members were shattered in 1987. One was that support for the Alliance had ceased to be regarded merely as a form of protest. Another was that tactical voting had become fashionable, and would operate in the Alliance's favour. In the by-elections of 1983–7 there had been much circumstantial evidence of tactical voting, and hopes had been expressed that the Alliance would pick up many general-election votes to ensure both Conservative and Labour defeats. Although the national decline in the Alliance's share of the vote in 1987 had been 2.8 per cent, in Labour-Alliance marginals the decline had been only about half that size, suggesting that some voters had supported Alliance candidates in order to prevent Labour winning. But in seats that were marginal between Conservative and Labour the decline was of the order of 4.4 per cent—a swing *away* from the Alliance to ensure Conservative victories.

During the 1987 election campaign the Alliance failed to dislodge Labour as the radical alternative to Thatcherism, but failed also to convince the electorate that it represented Thatcherism with a human face. This happened because the Alliance leaders were divided as to which enemy to pursue with most vigour—a lack of purpose that was reflected in the content of its manifesto, which attempted to be all things to almost all people: electoral reform (including fixed-term parliaments); better management of state education; massive investment to cut the jobless total by one million in three years; a commitment to 'make unions democratic and accountable'; qualified support for the sale of some state-owned industries; increased spending on the National Health Service; support for private health insurance; more statutory protection for the environment; a promise to institute an Animal Protection Commission; help for first-time home-buyers; more support for local-authority and private tenants; a commitment to a non-nuclear defence policy, but only within the framework of multilateral nuclear disarmament.

The shortcomings of the manifesto might have been accommodated and balanced by a strong leadership. This David Steel and David Owen (elected to succeed Roy Jenkins as SDP leader in 1983) failed to provide. According to the evidence of the BBC/Gallup survey, the major causes of defections among former Alliance voters in 1987 were the beliefs (a) that the Alliance had no chance of winning the election and (b) that voting Alliance would have led to the return of a Labour government. Among the 23 per cent of voters who seriously considered voting Alliance but did not do so, belief (a) also came top of the list, followed by (c) the conviction that one party should not have two leaders. The twin leadership of the Alliance was widely held to have been a major cause of public dissatisfaction with it. For although Steel himself turned out to be the most popular of the party leaders, more impressive, indeed, than Mrs Thatcher, what alienated public opinion in 1987 was the failure of Steel and Owen to impress *as a team*.

It is a truism that British general elections have become much more presidential in style, with a great deal of media attention focused on the Prime Minister and the potential Prime Minister. The Alliance appeared to offer *two* potential Prime Ministers and—worse still—two whose differences became ever more apparent as the campaign progressed. The Alliance campaign failed, therefore, at two levels. First, there was a failure to identify one enemy and attack it consistently. Secondly, the electors were treated to the public spectacle of a fundamental difference between the leaders of the Alliance as to who the enemy really was.

In the early days of the campaign the Alliance mounted an onslaught against Thatcherite Conservatism, especially on the issue of unemployment. But it soon became clear that David Owen's heart was not in this strategy. On 19 May he told an audience in Norwich that the Conservative government lacked compassion and that its policies had damaged national unity; none the less, he declared, the Prime Minister was entitled to 'her share of plaudits' for the necessary reforms that she had pushed through. A few days later, when it was becoming clear that anti-Thatcherism was resulting in the loss of Alliance support to the Conservatives, there was a change of strategy. Owen and Shirley Williams became more outspoken in their attacks on Labour, in the context of the influence of the hard left. Owen counselled a Cambridge audience against playing the Labour game 'of painting her [Mrs Thatcher] as the Prime Minister of unmitigated woe', and he warned against Labour's unilateralist defence policy and its attitude towards the police, trade unions, and the role of private enterprise in economic recovery. Television audiences were left in no doubt that David Owen regarded Labour as the greater threat to the national interest.

In the last full week of the campaign, when there was talk of a hung Parliament, Owen confessed that he would much prefer to support a minority Conservative government than a minority Labour one. David Steel, however, had compared Mrs Thatcher to Arthur Scargill. He objected to the 'extremely authoritarian' manner in which the Conservative government treated its citizens, and he made it abundantly clear (4 June) that he was not 'going to be part of the Thatcher government', by supporting it in the event of a parliamentary stalemate. Members of the Liberal Party made no secret of their displeasure at what they regarded as the pro-Tory bias of the SDP leader. By the eve of the poll it was clear that the Alliance had fallen apart. David Owen had chosen the right target, but David Steel refused to press home the attack.

The election result made it inevitable that the days of the Alliance were numbered. Owen had already hinted at this at the beginning of June. Had there been a hung Parliament, the SDP leader might have been in a position to remodel the Alliance according to his own blueprint. In fact, not only was Alliance representation diminished in the new House of Commons, the SDP was reduced to a rump of five (Owen himself, Rosie Barnes, Robert Maclennan, John Cartwright and Charles Kennedy), compared with 17 Liberals; Shirley Williams and Bill Rodgers had failed to secure election, and Roy Jenkins had been defeated. In the ensuing inquest, all sections of the Alliance coalition were panicked into frankly unrealistic positions.

Alliance voters, on the evidence of a MORI poll, favoured a fusion of the Liberals with the SDP. Most Liberals also supported such an amalgamation, which would rid the 'third force' in English politics of the apparatus of dual control with which the electors had clearly been unimpressed. David Steel saw in such a merger the foundation of a much wider anti-Thatcherite coalition, hoping still for that fundamental realignment on the left that had—and has—proved so illusive. Had the Labour Party suffered *very* badly in 1987, such a hope might have been justified. In fact, as we have seen, Labour did not do well, but was able to rely on core regional support to ensure its survival and credibility; Mr Kinnock remained Leader of Her Majesty's Opposition, while most of the Labour MPs who had deserted to the SDP had emerged from the 1987 contest with their parliamentary careers in ruins.

Supporters of Lib-Labism (1980s version) have pointed out that an electoral arrangement between the Labour Party and the Liberals, reminiscent of that agreed in 1903, would have resulted in a Conservative defeat. Calls for such a pact have come from Labour intellectuals, such as Professor Bernard Crick, and from some Labour MPs, and it is pointed out that the price the Liberals would be bound to exact—proportional representation and devolution—is one that a significant section of the Labour movement might be willing to pay:

> The difficulty of getting Liberal voters to vote Labour will be overcome [R.W. Johnson, of Magdalen College, Oxford, wrote in *The Times*, 7 July 1987] by Labour conceding proportional representation. This will not only provide an irresistible carrot to Liberal voters, but will offer a future in which the Liberals will be securely independent of Labour.

To argue along these lines is to put logic at the service of fantasy. Before the First World War the franchise was very restricted. Labour had no hope of becoming a mass party; many MPs elected under the Labour banner were, in fact, Liberals. The very limited—and secret—arrangement entered into in 1903 did not result in a coalition government. In any case, it needs to be borne in mind that 80 years ago there was an identity of interests between Liberals and the non-socialist Labour Party that went beyond the immediate desire to prevent the Conservatives from retaining or gaining office. Today very different considerations apply. We cannot argue with the statement that the 1987 general election proved that an anti-Thatcherite majority exists among the voting population. The problem is that the political parties which, between them, represent this majority are, doctrinally, worlds apart.

In eight hectic months following the 1987 election the nature of the Alliance was fundamentally altered; what has resulted is a merged party that could not possibly put itself forward as a creature of the left. The call to merge came from David Steel, and had few dissentients within the Liberal Party, which voted for it by 2,099 votes to 385 at a special Assembly held in Blackpool on 23 January 1988. On the Liberal side the way had been smoothed by a remarkable autumn 1987 Conference at Harrogate, where the unilateralism espoused by Liberals in 1986 (but not reflected in the 1987 Alliance manifesto) was unceremoniously cast aside. What emerged was a set of policies little different from those of the Tory 'Wets' that Mrs Thatcher has been gradually dismissing from her government: opposition to 'mindless privatisation', so that basic utilities (such as water and electricity) would be kept in the public sector; more freedom for private enterprise from Whitehall control; the abandonment of a statutory incomes policy, and of what Richard Holme (adviser to David Steel) called 'gadgets' such as a counter-inflation tax; the explicit rejection of any hint of unilateralist tendencies; a greater emphasis upon national efficiency, and a greater willingness to trust business and commerce to produce this efficiency while preserving a compassionate society. In short, the Liberal Party ceased being a party offering a better collectivism than Labour, and became instead a party committed to a more caring individualism and enterprise culture than the Conservatives.

These values are demonstrably 'Owenite'. But David Owen, Rosie Barnes and John Cartwright refused to hitch themselves to the wagon that had been so carefully repainted for them. On the SDP side the road to merger was paved with nails. Owen yielded the leadership to Robert Maclennan (6 August 1987), and fought on, claiming to be the guardian of true Social Democracy, even though a special party Conference later that month endorsed the principle of merger overwhelmingly. The new Social and Liberal Democrats (SLD) came into being in 1988 in a welter of squabbling, abuse, bitterness, legal action and general confusion, symbolised by the presentation and hasty retraction of a policy 'prospectus' which had, out of deference to the SDP (and perhaps in an effort to tempt the Owenites out of their secessionist mood), praised Mrs Thatcher for having 'strengthened the spirit of enterprise and self-reliance and curbed abuses of union power . . . She deserves credit for nerve [the document said] but not for judgment'.

There is, understandably, a great deal of voter confusion about the relationship between the Democrats and the Owenite SDP. At the May 1988 local elections both parties suffered from the fact that in well over 100 wards Democrat and SDP candidates fought each other as well as the Labour and Conservative contenders. However, although both wings of the former Alliance lost roughly half the gains they had made in 1984, it was the SDP which suffered worst. It now has no more than a toe-hold on local government, and its credibility may suffer as a result. But the Democrats, with 20 per cent of the vote (as measured in the 1988 local-election results), clearly has a future of sorts. What shape that future may take can only be dimly perceived.

The fate of the policy prospectus is, however, illuminating. It included firm support for NATO and the Trident nuclear-missile system, a commitment to nuclear power stations, the replacement of the system of universal child benefit by one that discriminated in favour of the genuinely needy, the phasing out of mortgage tax relief, and the investigation of proposals to extend VAT to food, children's clothing, domestic fuel and newspapers. Liberal Party members and Liberal MPs exploded with wrath at what they regarded as the betrayal of Liberal principles, such as no taxation of food and knowledge; Michael Meadowcroft, a former Liberal MP and president-elect of the Liberal Party, pointed to its Quaker traditions and explained that his conscience would not permit the inclusion of a commitment to NATO in the constitution of the new party, though he did not object to a commitment to 'collective security with our allies' — which (when one thinks about it) amounts to much the same thing.[3]

These differences did not prevent the emergence of the new party, nor will they — of themselves — prevent its growth. Party programmes (especially the programmes of opposition parties) are, in any case, shaped to a large extent by national circumstances. Opposition to NATO is confined to the lunatic fringe of the British political system. The 1987 Alliance manifesto envisaged no immediate need for more nuclear power stations, but it did include a pledge to continue research into 'nuclear fission power'. Trident will, by the time of the next general election, be a fact of life. The harmonisation of tax systems within the European Community (to whose well-being generations of loyal Liberals have been committed) may well lead to the extension of VAT to books, newspapers and clothing, and it is possible that, also by the time of the next general election, the present arrangements for child benefit and mortgage tax relief will have been drastically modified by the Thatcher government.

The merged Democrats will overcome their early teething troubles over policy, and, under their new leader, Paddy Ashdown, they will no doubt be able to appeal to the so-called centre ground, whose borders now lie far to the right of those to be observed 30 years ago. If the Democrats really do espouse unilateralism, they are doomed to everlasting opposition; but if they turn their backs on unilateralism once and for all, and lose some unilateralists to Labour, their leaders will be right to consider this no bad thing. The more socialist Labour becomes, the better will be the prospects, not so much for a Democrat government, but certainly for Democrat participation in a coalition should the events of 1974 repeat themselves.

For the Owenites the outlook is bleak. We can of course sympathise at once with their feeling of betrayal, and we can understand how they have come to the view that they were enticed into the original SDP deliberately as a half-way house to merger with the Liberals. Should the Democrats do a deal with Labour, David Owen's rump SDP might acquire new support 'on the rebound'. But to stake the future of a political party on such a chance is to take a desperate gamble. Moreover, unless and until such a day arrives, the Owenite SDP must live within an electoral environment of general hostility.

Shortly after his resignation as SDP leader, in August 1987, David Owen wrote that 'The SDP was deliberately created as a fourth party. Those who believe that there is only room for three-party politics in Britain are making a profound mistake'.[4] Had such words been penned by anyone else, we would have to conclude that they were the views of a political ignoramus, someone suffering from the hallucination that proportional representation already existed in Britain. Dr Owen is certainly not a political ignoramus, but he does appear to be so blinded by his own lofty ideals, and so obsessed by his own belief in the reality of a 'hard centre', able (he says) to force a referendum on PR, that the harsh realities of British politics at the end of the 1980s appear to have escaped his attention.

The new Democrats will occupy the hard centre-ground, acting as a refuge for the battered of the right and the left, worrying less about political consistency than about political survival. The Owenites may well remain consistent; but power will elude them. The best hope that Dr Owen has of ever again influencing the course of British politics is to join or at least support the Conservative Party, as other respectable non-doctrinaire radicals (such as Winston Churchill and Joseph Chamberlain) have done without embarrassment. Mrs Thatcher admires guts and courage, especially when displayed in the service of the crusade against socialism; she would welcome the Owenites and she might just be persuaded to honour their leader with a place in her government.[5]

NOTES

1. A. Heath, R. Jowell & J. Curtice (1985), *How Britain Votes*, Oxford, Pergamon Press, p. 151.
2. P. Zenter, (1982), *Social Democracy in Britain*, London, John Martin, pp. 195, 197; the emphasis is mine.
3. *The Times*, 14 January 1988.
4. *Sunday Times*, 9 August 1987.
5. The flattering remarks made about Dr Owen by Mrs Thatcher, interviewed by Brian Walden in the *Sunday Times*, 8 May 1988, seem particularly significant in this regard. The result of the Richmond (Yorkshire) by-election (23 February 1989) appeared to have given the Owenites a new lease of life, since their candidate pushed the Democrats into third place and came within 3,000 votes of capturing the seat from the Conservatives. We should note, however, that much of the credit for this performance must go to the personal popularity of the Owenite candidate (a local farmer), who built upon particular circumstances that are unlikely to be replicated in many other English constituencies.

4. Conservatism: The Art of Survival

The survival of the Conservative Party over 150 years of steady democratisation of the British political system is, by any standards, little short of astonishing. A party that traces its origins to the defence of aristocratic privilege has flourished into an age of apparent social and political equality. A party whose roots were — quite literally — to be found in the land, in the agricultural interests of the late eighteenth and nineteenth centuries, has presided over industrial growth and has come to be seen as the champion of business and commercial enterprise. A party whose stubborn refusal to embrace even the most modest proposals for parliamentary reform (1830–2) brought the country within hailing distance of a revolution has willingly embraced populism as its watchword, pandering to the lowest and commonest denominators of mass appeal. Above all, a party that has always professed its adherence to unshakeable principles and beliefs has demonstrated an extraordinary ability to live for the moment, to forget today what it has preached yesterday.

Schoolchildren are taught that Sir Robert Peel was the founder of modern Conservatism. That Peel saved the party from oblivion cannot be doubted. Over Catholic Emancipation in 1829 and the repeal of the Corn Laws in 1846 Peel triumphed over the party die-hards, whose excessive zeal for various outmoded causes (anti-Catholicism, dating from the late seventeenth century, and the protection of British agriculture, dating from the early nineteenth) threatened the very fabric of society. On both occasions, however, Peel committed a sin which Conservatives do not easily forgive: he put principle before party, causing deep divisions which, in the case of the Corn Laws, were never healed. Peel did what had to be done. But the Peelites, such as Gladstone, wedded to free trade and the gradual abolition of privilege (though not, it should be noted, to the idea of parliamentary democracy) were cast out of the party and forced to spend a decade and more in the wilderness before becoming part of a great coalition of more-or-less progressive forces known as Liberalism.

The leadership of the Conservative Party fell, by stages, upon Benjamin Disraeli, a brilliant orator, a novelist and (by birth at least) a Jew. Disraeli had few moral scruples about him, and his political principles were fewer still. But he had a nose for power; he knew where it lay now, and where it was to lie in the future. He was also motivated by an obsessive personal ambition. His spiteful attacks on Peel in the 1840s were ostensibly based upon his opposition to free trade. In fact they sprang from intense disappointment at having been denied a post in Peel's government. 'Protection', Disraeli told a friend in 1850, 'is not only dead, but damned', and he was never to attempt to resurrect it, not even in the 1870s, when imports of cheap American grain caused British farmers real hardship and when, as head of a government with a comfortable majority in both Houses of Parliament, he could have done so.

In Disraeli most Conservatives felt confident that they now possessed a leader under whom the Land and the Church would not be further compromised, and under whom the stresses of an increasingly industrial society would be kept in check. Disraeli, for his part, sat uneasily at the head of the party. He told his followers what they wanted to hear: that the objects of the party were still 'to maintain the institutions of the country . . . [and] . . . the Empire of England' (speech at the Crystal Palace, 24 June 1872). He also referred to the need to elevate 'the condition of the people'. His great ministry of 1874–80 did indeed pass a certain amount of social-reforming legislation, primarily in the fields of working-class housing, merchant shipping and industrial relations. It was by Disraeli's hand, and that of his industrious Home Secretary R.A. Cross, that trade unions were liberated from the rigours of the criminal law, and that the first real steps were taken to deal with the jerry-built slums of the industrial revolution.

Disraeli's claim to have established modern Conservatism is certainly greater then Peel's. While maintaining the party's aristocratic traditions, and its devotion to the Land, he helped it come to terms with the realities of an urban, industrial state by pointing it in the direction of an alliance with the skilled artisans—the Victorian working-class aristocracy—*against* the get-rich-quick industrial bourgeoisie for whom the Liberal Party acted as political mouthpiece. That is not to say that he trusted the working classes. He did not. The second Reform Act (1867), which enfranchised working-class, male heads of households living in the towns, was, in its details, an accident. Disraeli (whose government at that time lacked an overall majority in the Commons) introduced an exceedingly moderate measure, in which a limited extension of the franchise was to be balanced by the giving of extra votes to those with money or university education enough to qualify for them.

Once introduced, however, the Bill was radically amended, so that the electorate of the United Kingdom was practically doubled. Old-guard Tories were furious. The future Conservative Prime Minister Lord Salisbury accused Disraeli of borrowing his principles 'from the ethics of the political adventurer'. We can agree that it was a gamble; but the gamble paid handsome dividends in the election victory of 1874, when a majority Conservative government was returned for the first time in over 30 years. In office Disraeli's domestic policies were largely cosmetic. The concessions to trade unions were real enough, but the Artisans' Dwellings Act was permissive (that is, it gave powers to local authorities to clear slums but did not compel them so to do), the Merchant Shipping Act was a farce (it forced shipowners to paint a maximum load line on every ship, but did not prevent the line being painted on the ship's funnel!), while the much-trumpeted Public Health Act of 1875 did no more than codify existing legislation.

None the less, in legislating along these lines Disraeli pointed Conservatism along the path of social reform, indicating, in a quite unashamedly paternalistic manner, that the party had a duty to care for those who could not look after themselves. In a fashion that was admittedly romantic, he did care about the division of Britain into 'Two Nations', and he genuinely regretted it. In this sense it might be argued that he was an egalitarian. He believed in equality under the law, in access for all to the opportunities, rights and obligations that society could provide. But he was blind to the fact that such access may in practice be denied by social inequality, by gross disparities of wealth and of the educational as well as the material resources that wealth can provide.

Disraeli's concern with social reform was carried forward after his death (1881) by Lord Randolph Churchill, whose recognition of the centrality of the working classes to the post-1867 electoral system led him to propose a radical extension of 'Tory Democracy'. Some of the measures enacted by Lord Salisbury's government of 1886–92 (e.g. free elementary education, further factory reform and the democratisation of county government) were the results of Churchill's legacy. But it was precisely at this time that the nature of the Conservative Party underwent a fundamental change, as a direct result of the desertion to it, from the Liberal Party, of a very significant section of the business classes. The last Conservative governments before the First World War, the administrations of Lord Salisbury (1895–1902) and of his nephew Arthur James Balfour (1902–5) were almost totally devoid of social-reforming content. The Workmen's Compensation Act of 1897 and the Education Act of 1902 were landmarks of their kind. But the local 'Distress Committees' set up under the 1905 Unemployed Workmen's Act were largely financed from private charity; the Aliens Act of the same year was nothing more that a sop to working-class xenophobia and antisemitism; and a very modest scheme for old-age pensions, to be paid to the needy and deserving poor over 65 years of age, was ruled out on the grounds that the cost of the Boer War precluded its implementation.

The revolt of property which had split the Gladstonian Liberal Party had profound repercussions upon Conservatism. Most of the Liberal Unionists who deserted Gladstone in 1886 were not radicals, but landowners and businessmen, profoundly distrustful of any attack upon wealth. The formal fusion of Liberal Unionists with Conservatives did not take place until 1912; but, certainly from 1895, the two groups formed a coherent political force dedicated to the protection of capital in any form and to the maintenance, in so far as it was possible, of the *status quo*. Henceforth the business community looked to Conservatism for its defence. By 1900 less than half the Conservative MPs were drawn from the ranks of the landed classes; 53 per cent of the parliamentary party in the Commons had industrial and professional backgrounds. Even then, the party was still heavily Anglican and led by a landed aristocrat who sat in the Lords. A dozen years later its leadership was entrusted to Andrew Bonar Law, an iron merchant from Glasgow and the son of a Presbyterian minister.

Conservatism had thus been reconstituted. In the short term this posed serious problems affecting the party's ability to win votes and form governments. Two traditions—the older home-grown aristocratic paternalism and the much newer, imported bourgeois ethic of individualism—vied with each other for dominance, while a third—imperialism—seemed to have a life of its own. Much of the expansion of Empire that took place under Disraeli (especially in Africa) was due to local initiatives over which the government in London had, in truth, little control. The Boer War (which after a heroic start deteriorated into a series of squalid guerrilla campaigns and the building of concentration camps) did the party little good at home: at the so-called 'Khaki' election of October 1900 the Conservative vote actually fell compared with 1895, although the national weakness of the Liberal Party assured Lord Salisbury a still splendid victory.

In 1903 Joseph Chamberlain, the Colonial Secretary, attempted to harness the idea of Empire to the growing demands of the business community, for protection against foreign imports, by calling for 'tariff reform'—free trade within the Empire coupled with fiscal retaliation against tariffs imposed by other governments on British goods. The idea was ahead of its time. The Conservative Party split, and the split was enough to ensure defeat at the general election of January 1906. The Conservatives were in opposition for the following nine years. Free trade continued for some considerable time to have a peculiar fascination for the British electorate; it was associated with the boom years of the mid-Victorian economy and, by implication, was held to have been responsible for them. In December 1923 Stanley Baldwin, who had succeeded Bonar Law as Prime Minister, called an election on the issue of protection—and lost. But the cause of Tariff Reform lived on, and triumphed in March 1932, when Joseph Chamberlain's son, Neville, obtained the approval of Parliament for a duty of 10 per cent on a wide range of imports from countries outside the Empire.

The abandonment of free trade did indeed mark the death of Liberal England; it also reflected the triumph of industrial interests within the Conservative Party. As a consequence, inter-war Conservatism was distinguished by a deep hostility to trade unionism and to the Labour Party. Industries that had been under state control during the Great War were handed back to their shareholders. The recommendation of a Royal Commission in 1919, that the coal mines be nationalised, was ignored. The advice of John Maynard Keynes, that Treasury money be used to stimulate the economy and create employment, was rejected. The so-called General Strike (in reality nothing more than a large-scale industrial dispute to obtain a measure of social justice for the miners) was defeated and, after its defeat, a Trade Disputes Act was passed (1927) that declared illegal any general or sympathetic strike, prohibited civil servants from joining a TUC-affiliated union, and replaced the principle of allowing a member of a trade union to 'contract out' of the union's political levy by 'contracting in', the hope (which was borne out) being that there would be a drastic fall in Labour Party membership and income as a result.

Yet, in spite of espousing and implementing policies that were clearly inimical to the interests of the manual working classes, and in spite of the fact that after 1928 Britain enjoyed, virtually, universal manhood and womanhood suffrage (most men and women aged 21 years and over being able to vote), the 1930s belonged to the Conservative Party. The National Governments of Ramsay MacDonald (1931–5), Stanley Baldwin (1935–7) and Neville Chamberlain (1937–40) were arguably the most popular governments this century, winning (at the elections of 1931 and 1935) well over half the total votes cast; they were also—overwhelmingly—Conservative governments. Some of the explanation for this paradox lies in the fact of a divided and weak opposition. But the explanation is also to be found in the remarkable strength —indeed renaissance—of Tory paternalism.

Tory paternalism survived primarily owing to the resilience of aristocratic traditions which, in the temper of the age, acquired a radical dimension of their own. Why did these traditions survive within a Conservative Party now given over largely to the further-ance of business norms? Because, quite simply, there was nowhere else for them to go. Tory Anglicans, like Lord Hugh Cecil (Salis-bury's son, born 1869), saw the pursuit of social justice as an act of religious faith, a sacred obligation towards the poor and the deprived. He was not ashamed to admit that Conservatism, therefore, 'must often itself be in sympathy at least with some of the objects of Socialism . . . tender to the sufferings of humanity, but scrupulous of the obligations of justice' (*Conservatism*, 1912). In the 1930s Quintin Hogg (later Lord Hailsham, born 1907), professed a belief in 'publicly-organised social services' (*The Accept-able Face of Western Civilisation*, 1973).

Either through genuine distress at the social deprivation they saw around them, or through fear of the breeding-ground this provided for the doctrines of revolution, Conservatives interested themselves in the notion of economic planning. In 1933 Harold Macmillan (born 1894) published *Reconstruction: A Plea for a National Policy*, and the organisation Political & Economic Planning (founded two years earlier), brought together Conservative, Labour and Liberal politicians as well as businessmen, academics and civil servants who were interested in finding peaceful solu-tions to the country's economic and social problems. In *The Middle Way*, published in 1938, Macmillan warned of the dangers of unfettered free market forces: 'if capitalism had been conducted all along [he wrote] as if the theory of private enterprise were a matter of principle . . . we should have had a civil war long ago.'

But the true hero of inter-war Toryism was Neville Chamberlain, in whom the instincts of the man of business and the man of compassion formed a unique blend. Chamberlain has had what might justly be termed 'a bad press'; his reputation for bungling, blind diplomacy that led, via the Munich crisis, to the Second World War is, without doubt, well deserved. But had he died in 1937 he would have been remembered as a great social reformer. As Minister of Health under Baldwin he pushed on to the statute book no less than 25 bills, of which the most significant were the Widows', Orphans, & Old Age Contributory Pensions Bill (enacted 1925) and the mammoth Local Government Bill (enacted 1929), which swept away the Victorian Poor Law and transferred responsibility for the poor (and for hospitals) to the county and county-borough authorities.

Chamberlain believed in the concept of local government, of truly local control of local services. The Conservatives had created the county councils (including the London County Council) in

1888, and the London boroughs in 1899. In 1902 Balfour had endowed the education committees of the various local authorities in England and Wales with the right to control primary, secondary and technical education. Chamberlain's Act of 1929 gave to the county councils new areas of responsibility covering roads, town and country planning, public health, and maternity and child welfare. As Chancellor of the Exchequer, 1931–7, Chamberlain broke with Treasury orthodoxy by implementing budgets that were frankly inflationary; he borrowed money to finance debt repayments, and rescinded earlier cuts in unemployment pay and the pay of public servants. When the need to pay for rearmament forced him to raise income tax, he balanced this by appropriating the Road Fund revenue (i.e. car tax) and by slapping a new tax (the National Defence Contribution) on business profits—a move which delighted the socialists and cause a short-lived panic on the Stock Exchange!

An appreciation of the basic components of Conservative social policy in the 1920s and 1930s is important not merely because it demonstrates the continuity of concern with working-class issues, but also because it takes us some way towards an understanding of the growth of 'consensus' politics in the 1940s and 1950s. The Tories defeated the General Strike, but they did not deprive the trade unions of that immunity from civil actions for damages that had been granted in 1906. The Poor Law was replaced by the means test; but the embryonic welfare state created by the Liberals before the First World War was not destroyed; in some respects, indeed, it was extended. The restoration of the Gold Standard, in 1925, at the pre-war parity of $4.86 to the pound, served the interests of the banking community, and was carried out in callous disregard of the damaging effects it was bound to have on domestic employment prospects. Baldwin's answer to complaints that the $4.86 level would make exports more expensive was that, if that was the case, workers would have to accept wage cuts. But in 1932 he and and the party he led accepted the need to protect British industry against foreign competition.

What the pre-1939 Conservative Party did not accept was that taxpayers' money should be used to 'create' employment; or that the trade unions ought to be drawn into the process of government; or that the state should provide a system of welfare provision for all its citizens; or that it was right for the state to run utility industries that were essential to the national well-being but were, in private hands, under-capitalised and therefore inefficient. Around these bastions both wings of the party rallied to the defence of the *status quo*. But the bastions fell, rapidly, during the Second World War.

For this development Winston Churchill must take much of the praise, or blame. Churchill, Lord Randolph's son, was a most unorthodox Tory, a free-trader who had joined the Liberal Party in 1904 and had become, in turn, an ally of Lloyd George in the campaign for social reform and a Home Secretary under whose regime troops had been sent to areas of industrial unrest and had (at Llanelly and Liverpool) shot strikers dead. Yet, in spite of his marked antipathy to the trade-union movement, and his vehement denunciations of the General Strike, Churchill appreciated the strength of working-class attachment to trade unionism, and when he became Prime Minister in 1940 he was determined to harness this strength to the war effort. Ernest Bevin, leader of the Transport & General Workers' Union, was brought into the government to take charge of the Ministry of Labour and National Service, and given a Cabinet seat. Bevin made all strikes illegal; but, with government approval, he drew the trade unionists ever closer into the machinery of government, insisting that their presence alongside employers on Joint Production Committees was essential to the war effort—as of course it was.

The demands of war persuaded the Conservatives that their view of the welfare state must also change. Conservatives were in general lukewarm over the proposals of Sir William Beveridge, Chairman of the Unemployment Insurance Statutory Commission, for a system of family allowances, a national health service, and a universal contributory insurance scheme covering unemployment, old-age and widows' pensions and funeral grants. The financing of these schemes was a major source of worry; their ambitious open-endedness seemed frankly foolhardy. In a broadcast made in March 1943 Churchill warned against 'fairy tales'. Yet the proposals were accepted, in principle, because of their undoubted relevance to national morale.

The adoption of 'war socialism' had resulted from an egalitarian spirit which infected national life. Evacuation of the poor from bombed-out city centres had led to a much greater awareness of what urban poverty was all about. The ability of the state to alleviate the symptoms of deprivation could now no longer be doubted, while the placing of government contracts had proved that unemployment could be cured. In short, the Second World War generated a national consensus, which Churchill's Coalition government had to recognise. A Cabinet Committee on Reconstruction, whose members included R.A. Butler and Ernest Bevin, produced agreed plans for a national health service, a system of social-security provision, a policy of full employment and a housing policy. Butler's 1944 Education Act provided 'secondary education for all', within a national framework for which the government itself took responsibility. The Family Allowances Act of 1945 was also a product of the wartime Coalition.

By 1945 the broad outlines of what became known as the consensus politics of the 1950s had taken shape. Churchill admitted as much when the new parliament assembled after Attlee's election victory: 'Here and there [he told the House of Commons] there may be differences of emphasis or view, but in the main no Parliament has ever assembled with such a mass of agreed legislation.' The level of the consensus—the agreement between the Labour and Conservative Parties as to the content and direction of public policy—could have been higher. In particular, there was certainly no agreement on the scope and extent of public ownership. The *Industrial Charter*, adopted by the Conservatives in 1947, talked about the creation of 'a sphere of free enterprise which is on terms with authority and which reconciles the need for central direction with the encouragement of individual effort'. Some sections of the party, encouraged by the Beaverbrook press, branded this as a capitulation to socialism; but Butler and Macmillan were forthright in its defence, and the majority of Conservative MPs also supported it.

Conservative opposition to Labour's early nationalisation measures was to a great extent ritualistic, and was more concerned with the terms of compensation to shareholders than with the principle of compulsory acquisition of private property—a principle which the Tories had already conceded. The state of the coal-mining and railway and canal industries was such that many owners and shareholders were only too happy to be rid of confirmed loss-makers. Some of the other undertakings nationalised by the Attlee government, such as gas and electricity, were already under substantial municipal ownership; in particular, the wholesale distribution of electricity had for over 20 years been under the control of the state-owned Central Electricity Board, set up by Baldwin's government in 1926.

Conservative attacks on Labour's nationalisation programme sprang from two sources. First, from the feeling that it was the duty of the Opposition to oppose; thus, Churchill announced his acceptance of the principle of nationalising the Bank of England, but some of his parliamentary colleagues insisted on denouncing it. Second, from the belief that the nationalisation of efficient privately owned undertakings was neither morally nor politically sound. For these reasons the Conservatives opposed the public ownership of the iron and steel industries, and of road haulage, and when they regained office they set about reversing Labour legislation in these areas (1953); the following year, however, as if to emphasise that the Conservative approach to public ownership was pragmatic throughout, they legislated to bring about an important extension of public control, through the establishment of the United Kingdom Atomic Energy Authority.

The strength of national support for Labour in the late 1940s and early 1950s helped bolster the authority, within the Conservative Party, of consensus-minded Conservatives. Between 1945 and 1950

Labour did not lose a single by-election; and, as we have seen, the Conservative victory in 1951 was purely technical. In 1949 the Conservative Party Conference gave overwhelming approval to *The Right Road For Britain*, a document which accepted the concept of a welfare state and endorsed the need for full employment, which the 1950 party manifesto declared would be 'the first aim' of a future Conservative government. Privately, some senior Conservatives doubted the wisdom of the commitment to full employment, noting that without the deterrent effect of unemployment the working classes were certain to be encouraged in their quest for higher wages; they were won over by the argument that the political consequences of the abandonment of full employment were bound to be decidedly negative. In any case, the economic prosperity of the early 1950s, the disappearance of wartime controls on consumption (meat and butter were derationed in 1954 and coal in 1958), added to the feeling of well-being that pervaded national life, and which Macmillan and Butler were anxious to have associated with the Conservative cause.

The 1950s were the golden age of non-dogmatic vote-catching Conservatism. At the Ministry of Housing (1951–4) Macmillan pushed forward with an ambitious programme (actually fulfilled) to build 300,000 houses a year. This was made possible by an increase in the amount of Treasury subsidy to local authorities, from £22 to £35 per home; taxpayers' money was, in this way, used to help boost employment. Butler, now at the Exchequer, managed to reduce public expenditure (for example, by trimming food subsidies), but balanced this by imposing an excess profits tax. More generally, under the Conservatives there was no abandonment of the concept of a managed economy, or of the commitment of government to promote economic growth thereby.

Public expenditure on welfare services continued to increase, even when the national rate of economic growth slowed down. Again, not all Conservatives agreed with this approach. In January 1958 Peter Thorneycroft, who had succeeded to the Exchequer when Macmillan became Premier the previous year, proposed to reduce public spending by some £50 million; the Cabinet refused to back him and he, together with his junior ministers Enoch Powell and Nigel Birch, were forced to resign. Macmillan brushed aside these 'little local difficulties'. He had already reminded the electorate that 'most of our people have never had it so good' (20 July 1957). This was true. Thorneycroft was replaced by Derick Heathcoat Amory, whose tax-cutting strategy provided the foundation for Macmillan's great election victory of 1959.

One other aspect of the consensus of the 1950s is worthy of mention, because it supplied a further important dimension to the ability of post-war Conservatism to sail with the prevailing wind. There was no reversal of Labour's policy of abandoning the

Empire. The image of the Conservative Party as imperialistic as well as jingoistic relies for its strength upon a relatively short-lived flirtation with colonialism, lasting no more than the 30 or so years that separated Disraeli's accession to office from the downfall of Balfour's government (1874–1905). Little of the empire-building that took place during this period can be traced to deliberate policy initiatives emanating from Whitehall, with the major exception of the desire to occupy Egypt in order to protect British interests in the Suez Canal. Churchill's opposition to the granting of Dominion status to India was one of the factors that kept him in the political wilderness in the 1930s, but Britain's virtual bankruptcy in 1945 made the granting of independence to India, Pakistan, Ceylon and Burma after the war a foregone conclusion. The Suez adventure (1956) can in one sense be seen as the occasion for a battle of wills between the imperialist dreamers (the 'Suez Group') and the sober realists in the party. Eden's attempt to use military force to reverse the Egyptian nationalisation of the Suez Canal was, without doubt, enormously popular at home; but it amounted to an absurd attempt to resurrect a past that was long since dead, and a dangerous arousal of passions that could not be gratified.

Again, it was Macmillan who was best able to separate myth from reality. He accepted the new status of the Canal, and took steps to repair Britain's relations with the United States, whose abandonment of Eden's government had left Britain isolated and humiliated. By a deliberate policy he and the Colonial Secretary, Iain Macleod, hastened the dismantling of the Empire, presenting the process of dismemberment as a triumph and a sign of national strength rather than of weakness. Between 1957 and 1963 almost all Britain's former colonial territories in Africa were granted independence, together with the major possessions in the West Indies and Cyprus. Those who argued that the end of Empire would react unfavourably upon Conservative popularity at home were clearly proved wrong. Colonial territories with militant nationalist movements were a drain on national resources. As sovereign states their economic ties with Britain remained substantially unchanged.

For those who attached importance to such things, the replacement of the Empire by the Commonwealth substituted one source of pomp and circumstance by another. At the same time moves were made to replace an old consensus by a new one. Both the Labour and the Conservative Parties had kept aloof from the European Economic Community. As we have already noted, many in the Labour Party regarded it as little more than a device to further the interests of multinational corporations and to fund the French agricultural industry. On both side there was much opposition to the loss of national sovereignty that membership would entail, and to the undoubted fact that to join the EEC Britain would have turn its back on the Empire. Macmillan's *volte-face* was inspired by a mixture of political and economic considerations. He wished to ensure a continuity of British influence in the world now that the Empire was being wound up, and he saw merit in the effects upon British industry of having to cope with European competition. General de Gaulle's veto of the British application to join the Common Market (1963) was a blow to Conservative morale, and a short-term defeat. But in a little over four years a Labour government had taken the same decision to join—and had suffered the same rebuff. A new area of agreement between the two parties had been created in the process.

So it was that, during the 1950s, the Conservative Party, through a process of constant adjustment to prevailing national moods, turned itself—once more—into a natural party of government. To say this is not to assert that the governments of Churchill, Eden and Macmillan enjoyed unqualified popularity. Clearly they did not. There was widespread concern at the failure of the British economy to match that of its American and Continental competitors, whose annual growth rates soared as that of Britain declined. Unemployment remained low (under 2 per cent). However, Britain's share of world markets, which had stood at 25 per cent when Churchill became Prime Minister in 1951, fell to 15 per cent by the time Macmillan's premiership had come to an end in 1963. The remedy prescribed by Chancellor Selwyn Lloyd was to call for a 'pay pause' (July 1961–March 1962) which, though enforced in the public sector, was voluntary elsewhere. Such a policy was bound to arouse resentment, not least because it was easily evaded by those with industrial muscle to do so, while the weakest groups (such as teachers and nurses) lost out. Nor did the Selwyn Lloyd pay pause or the 'guiding light' of between 2 and 3.5 per cent that operated between 1962 and 1964 achieve their objectives. Throughout the entire period July 1961–October 1964 hourly wage rates increased by an annual average of 4.3 per cent. At the same time a series of deflationary budgets resulted in more unemployment, which reached 878,000 in February 1963.

Yet the option of allowing unemployment to reach its own natural level was never taken up. Not only would this have been politically unacceptable; it would have offended the patrician and humanistic values of the then Tory leadership, and challenged the claim of the party to be truly national, and not sectional or class-based. On the contrary, great care was taken to build bridges into the trade-union movement, and give union leaders a formal role in the evolution of a national economic strategy; this policy resulted in the establishment of the National Economic Development Council (NEDC), in 1961, upon which union representatives sat as of right.

But the setting-up of the NEDC—coming as it did just a few days after the publication of the Plowden Report on the Control of

Public Expenditure—had a much deeper significance. It was during the period of office of these Conservative governments that the first tentative steps were taken to give practical expression to the idea of economic planning, to which the previous Labour administration had paid no more than lip-service. In his budget of 1956 Macmillan argued that over-employment was creating excessive demand in the economy, resulting in higher price levels and a higher volume of imports. But he deliberately set his face against deflation through restricting demand, because of its impact on employment. Incomes policies—however crudely operated and however unsuccessful—were also designed as a planned reaction to economic problems. Forecasts of demand could not be made for periods longer than two years; it was imperative that economic strategy be considered over a much longer time-span. The Conservatives managed to secure the approval in principle of both sides of industry to this approach, a remarkable extension of the consensus model when we remember that in the view of many industrialists national economic planning was a socialist device.

Once this threshold had been crossed, it was much easier to obtain broad approval within the Conservative Party to genuinely interventionist economic policies. The party Conferences of 1962 and 1963 exhibited a warmth towards planning that had been noticeably absent hitherto, perhaps because the concept of planning could be dovetailed into that of modernisation, a theme which the Labour opposition under its new leader, Harold Wilson, was now ruthlessly exploiting in the service of its anti-government propaganda. Certainly by 1964 the Conservatives were concerned much less about the legitimacy of planning than about its scope and extent. On this point the 1964 Tory manifesto was unambiguous: 'the NEDC [it said] gives reality to the democratic concept of planning by partnership. In contemporary politics the argument is not for or against planning. All human activity involves planning. The question is: how is the planning to be done? By consent or by compulsion?'

The election of 1964 marked a watershed in the history of the relationship between Conservatism and consensus. For 25 years from 1940 the party had moved steadily towards what it perceived as the new centre-ground in British politics and society, where a welfare state had been built on the foundations of full employment and a substantial publicly owned industrial sector, and upon which the government, in partnership with management and unions, planned for national economic growth. The occupation of this centre-ground had given the Conservatives three successive (and successively more sweeping) election victories.

The embrace of the consensus involved sacrifices of previously held principles, especially that which related to the benefits of a free-market economy. By 1964 only one Conservative of the first rank remained who dared to extol these benefits in public, namely Enoch Powell, who (it will be recalled) had resigned his Treasury post in 1958 on the issue of limiting public spending. Powell held ministerial office again (at the head of the Department of Health) between 1960 and 1963, but he refused to serve in the government of Sir Alec Douglas-Home (1963–4) and, once the party was in opposition after 1964, he led a crusade against high public spending, economic planning and incomes policies. Powell was also an inveterate opponent of British entry into the Common Market, arguing (rightly) that membership of the EEC would involve fundamental and far-reaching limitations upon British sovereignty and the supremacy, within the United Kingdom, of the Westminster Parliament; and he warned, in sensational terms, of the allegedly adverse consequences of Black immigration.

Powell has sometimes been portrayed as a shining example of a principled politician, basing his actions on a set of fundamental doctrines grounded in libertarian values. In fact, a true disciple of free trade would have argued against any restriction on immigration, because such restriction protects domestic wage-levels; immigration laws act, in other words, as a form of protective tariff. However, Powellites saw in the immigration issue a new source of support for the Conservative Party, both in itself and because the issue proved an embarrassment for Labour. Under Mrs Thatcher the Conservatives have exploited this issue to the full. But in the 1960s it was hoped that there could be a bi-partisan approach from the major political parties, and that the subject might, somehow, be 'taken out of politics'. Powell's mistake was to have spoken too stridently and too soon. In the first-ever election of a Conservative Leader, in 1965, Powell had stood in order to see how much support there might be among Conservative MPs for old-fashioned *laissez-faire* economics. There was, in truth, very little: Powell came bottom of the poll with only 15 votes. Although a member of the Shadow Cabinet, his increasing obsession with Black immigration made him a liability, and in 1968 Heath dismissed him.

But it would be wrong to conclude from this episode that the election of Heath signified a determination to shore up the consensus of the 1950s and launch it, intact, into the politics of the 1970s. Our view of Heath's period as Conservative Leader (1965–75) is heavily coloured by the Thatcherite reaction to and revulsion against it. This reaction is easily understood. The four years of Conservative rule under Heath contained elements of the tragic as well as of the farcical. The 1970 Conservative manifesto, *A Better Tomorrow*, had stated: 'We will stop further nationalisation'; yet Rolls-Royce was nationalised by the government after only eight months in office. The manifesto had also stated: 'We utterly reject the philosophy of compulsory wage control'; such a philosophy was implemented in November 1972. Attempts to hold down inflation foundered when, in the aftermath of renewed conflict in the Middle East (October 1973), much higher charges for imported food, raw materials and oil had a devastating impact on the cost of living. Heath succeeded at last in negotiating the United Kingdom's entry into the Common Market (1973), but he split his own party in the process and the benefits of entry (overtaken as it was by the great inflation later in the year) were not immediately apparent.

There was a thorough-going and long overdue reform of local government (1972) and, the following year, of the National Health Service, but these important reforms did not grip the public imagination: like Heath himself they exuded dullness. Above all, the government proved itself astonishingly weak in confronting the trade unions. The 1971 Industrial Relations Act was wrecked by the determination of the TUC to frustrate its implementation, and the miners proved a constant thorn in the government's side, penetrating ever deeper and sapping its will to govern. Heath need not have called an election on 28 February 1974, and even supposing the outcome had been a Conservative victory, it is difficult to see how this, of itself, would have brought the miners' strike to an end.

Thatcherites too easily condemn Heath for having committed the cardinal sin of compromise, forgetting that under Macmillan's influence it was the quite unashamed and unapologetic practice of compromise that had proved such a successful recipe for prolonged public support. Heath's tenure of the leadership coincided (as we noted in Chapter One) with a re-ordering of class-party alignments and a weakening of partisan commitment. Harold Wilson had sensed this, and had attempted to move Labour's focus of interests away from Clause 4 and unilateralism to the modernisation of industry and the efficient management of the mixed economy, in which was included statutory control of prices and wages and an attempted draconian reform of the trade unions. On the Conservative side Heath endeavoured also to modernise party policy. His failure was related much more closely to the practical application of new policies than to their formulation.

Thatcherite Conservatism was indeed built upon the Heath experiment. The Heath period marked a decisive break with the politics of consensus that Conservatives had pursued so doggedly hitherto. The very fact of Heath's election was an indication of the wind of change that was sweeping over the party. Under Macmillan and Home the social composition of the Conservative Party remained narrowly elitist; the parliamentary party was drawn heavily from the upper- middle classes, a true old-boy network of which the commercial elements were very happily a part; in the 1950s about three-quarters of the parliamentary party had attended public schools, but less than two-thirds had had a university education, and, more remarkably, less than one-third had business backgrounds. Twenty-one of the 24 members of the Home Cabinet of 1963 had attended a public school; eleven of these had gone to Eton alone. At its base the party could claim a membership that was one-third working class; most of the remainder were lower-middle class, such as teachers and small shopkeepers. But this reasonably egalitarian state of affairs disappeared as one moved from members to office-holders. Most local Conservative Party officials were drawn from the professional and managerial classes (who formed less than 5 per cent of the electorate); but even they, in turn, were under-represented in the parliamentary party.

Even before the defeat of 1964 party managers had voiced their concern that this state of affairs was bound to put an unacceptable distance between the party and the electorate. Gaitskell's attempt to make the Labour Party change course failed partly because of the diffusion of power within the party, the constitutional strength of the party Conference and the role of the NEC. The structure of the Conservative Party made the task of reform much less tedious. The National Union of Conservative & Unionist Associations has a mass membership but no formal role in policy-making; working- and lower-middle-class sentiments can be expressed at the party Conference—the Conference of the National Union—but the party Leader is protected if these sentiments do not accord with his or her own. The National Union has a Central Council, but this only meets once a year and is no way comparable to Labour's NEC.

Conservative Central Office (the party's London headquarters), the Conservative Political Centre (dispensing information and propaganda) and the Conservative Research Department are all under the control of the party Leader. Remarkably—and in the name of democracy—the powers of the Leader have been steadily augmented since the Second World War: greater democratisation and accountability have been imposed on the party from the top, to serve the interests of the leadership; they have not originated with the grass-roots. For example, the acceptance of the Maxwell-Fyfe report in the late 1940s put a stop to the 'buying' of constituency nominations by aspiring Conservative candidates, but also gave Central Office the power to suggest candidates and to approve those chosen by local Associations.

The adoption of an elective system for the choice of Conservative Leader, in 1965, actually resulted in an erosion of the influence of the grass-roots in what had admittedly been a furtive and ill-defined process hitherto, Before 1965 'the customary processes of consultation' (Macmillan's phrase) led to the election (in practice, by acclamation) of the Leader at a meeting of Conservative peers, MPs, candidates and National Union officials. Now Tory MPs alone have the right to make this choice. And, once they have done so, the Leader so chosen is free of any formal control or moderation. He or she appoints the party Chairman, the Vice-Chairman, the party Treasurer, the Directors of Central Office and of the Research Department, and all other party officers. All statements of party policy, including the election manifesto, are likewise promulgated on the sole authority of the Leader. Of course, in exercising these powers any sensible leader will take soundings and listen carefully to advice. But there is no obligation to take notice of what is said.

Strictly speaking, therefore Tory Democracy is a sham democracy. But it has the virtue that it enables a radical leader to propel the party in new and, perhaps, hitherto forbidden directions, without having to worry too much about intra-party dissent. The coalition of business, property and religious interests that make up the party membership can be leap-frogged in the wider interests of consolidating and expanding the party's national appeal. At the end of the day the only question that matters is: has the popularity of the party been enhanced thereby? If the answer is in the affirmative, little else matters, because in politics (as in show-business) nothing succeeds like success.

So it came to pass that it was a Conservative government, in 1954, that legislated to permit commercial television to function in Britain in the teeth of opposition from the Church of England, professional educationalists and a sizeable body of Conservative backbenchers, who complained (rightly) that the measure had never featured in the 1951 Conservative manifesto and (more questionably) that its passage into law was therefore unconstitutional. A powerful commercial lobby (the Popular Television Association) converted Central Office and the Cabinet to its view; the resultant pressure was irresistible. The inauguration of commercial television ran counter to the majority recommendations of the Beveridge Committee on Broadcasting (1947–9) and was opposed by the Labour Party. In this sense it might be defined as anti-consensual. But its appeal could not be doubted; it was a vote-winner. Its triumph reflected the renewed strength of large business interests within the Conservative world.

This strength was demonstrated again, in a manner that was less dramatic but more significant in terms of the future direction of Conservative policy, in January 1964, when the then President of the Board of Trade—none other than Edward Heath—announced that the Conservative government intended to legislate to prohibit (with certain exceptions) the system whereby manufacturers and wholesalers required retailers to abide by minimum price levels for the sale of their products.

The battle over resale price maintenance (RPM) was fought largely *within* the Conservative Party, between an alliance of established vested interests comprising manufacturers, wholesalers and retailers—especially small 'street-corner' shopkeepers—

and a newer, aggressive and financially well-endowed coalition of large retail chains and discount houses, the shopkeepers of the future. Heath appeared as the consumers' champion, offering competition and choice, and an end to retail price levels which were generally acknowledged to be artificially high.

Legislating RPM (with some exceptions) out of existence was a calculated risk: it alienated a set of interests whose support had, for the past half-century at least, been of central importance to the survival and growth of the Conservative Party. It demonstrated a flexibility of approach that could not be matched on the Labour side; at the same time, as a lesson in practical populism, it fell squarely within Conservative traditions. It also gave a clue as to the direction in which the party would be taken under Heath's leadership.

Immediately following the defeat of 1964 moves were set in train to give positions of responsibility to younger elements in the party. Brendan Sewill became, at the age of 35, Director of the Research Department and David Howell, aged 28, was put in charge of the Political Centre, which was brought more closely under Central-Office control. In January 1965 the party acquired a new Chairman, Edward du Cann, a man of the City, then 40 years of age, who had been a junior minister at the Board of Trade. Though educated at Oxford, du Cann had not been to a public school. Nor had Edward Heath, the 49-year-old grammar-school and Oxford-educated son of a well-to-do carpenter. Heath and du Cann possessed no trace of that sentimental attachment to the virtues of the middle-ground that had characterised the Conservative leadership over the previous 20 years. That is not to say that they rejected the 'One Nation' approach bequeathed by Disraeli. They simply refused to believe that One Nation could be achieved without a large injection of old-fashioned managerial efficiency and enterprise.

Under Heath and du Cann the Conservative Party experienced two revolutions. The first was organisational, and in its origins predated the accession to power of the new leadership. Du Cann put into effect the major recommendations of a report by Lord Chelmer into the role of constituency agents, who were henceforth expected to take a much higher political profile, for which they were to be given suitable education. There was also a thoroughgoing examination of the list of approved parliamentary candidates, with the object of reducing the number of peers, landowners and military gentlemen. At first this review had little impact. Constituency associations are independent bodies, whom Central Office may persuade but cannot usually coerce. In 1966 there were ten fewer old Etonians among the totality of Conservative candidates than there had been in 1964; otherwise the educational pattern of these candidates was much the same as before. But by the mid-1970s some significant changes (reflected in Table 4.1) were under way.

Table 4.1 Education and occupation of Conservative candidates, 1964 and October 1974

	Elected		Defeated		Total	
	1964	**1974**	**1964**	**1974**	**1964**	**1974**
Secondary and university	29	41	68	89	97	130
Public school only	63	59	81	62	124	121
Public school and university	141	149	124	117	265	266
Professions	94	91	143	116	237	207
Armed services	19	8	16	5	35	13
Teachers	4	12	21	27	25	39
Business	75	91	44	137	119	228

Source: adapted from D. Butler & A. King, *The British General Election of 1966* (Macmillan, 1966) and D. Butler & D. Kavanagh, *The British General Election of October 1974* (Macmillan, 1975).

The proportion of candidates from the 'prestige' public schools — Eton, Harrow and Winchester — was in decline; candidates educated at secondary schools and universities had increased by a third; and those with business backgrounds had almost doubled. Although, therefore, the public-school element remained dominant throughout the Heath era, there were many more Conservative MPs with company backgrounds at the end of it than when he became Leader. In 1964 businessmen accounted for only a quarter of the entire Conservative parliamentary party; a decade later the proportion had increased to a third.

More sweeping, however, was the review of policy that Heath and du Cann initiated. In October 1964 Heath had assumed the chairmanship of the party's Advisory Committee on Policy. Gaitskell had made the mistake of attempting to revise Labour policy by proposing alterations to its underlying philosophy. In his re-directing of Conservative policy, Heath did not fall into this error. Conservative principles — whatever they might then have been — were side-stepped. Instead, there was a searching reappraisal of specific policy areas. Mindful that such a review could well encounter resistance from party officials used to the old ways, Heath recruited a band of MPs, business and professional people, and academics (a group whose advice Conservatives had generally shunned hitherto, but whose impact as opinion-formers was then considerable). By the spring of 1965 no less than 36 'advisory groups' had been established. The collective results of their labours—a document entitled *Putting Britain Right Ahead*—was presented to the party Conference in October 1965.

Putting Britain Right Ahead broke—definitively—with the post-war consensus. Its underlying theme was that the universality of the welfare state had created a quite unbearable burden, which the national economy could no longer support. Personal taxation sapped incentive, while company taxation bore too heavily upon the private sector. In order to reduce government expenditure, therefore, and levels of direct taxation, the welfare state would have to become more selective in choosing those whom it assisted; this implied much more means-testing of those who alleged they were in need. However, some of the cost of social services would be transferred from the Treasury to individual employers, who would benefit from the implied encouragement to make more efficient use of their labour force. In a significant reference to the fate of the state graduated pensions scheme, *Putting Britain Right Ahead* argued that this would become a residual scheme for 'those relatively few' who would not, in the course of time, be covered by occupational (generally employer-provided) pension arrangements.

The document also made reference to the desirability of Britain entering the Common Market at 'the first favourable opportunity' and, meanwhile, urged a gradual end to the system of agricultural subsidies. But its major contribution to the debate about industrial organisation was to demand extensive trade-union reform, most notably the setting up of a new system of industrial courts to settle disputes and to enforce certain types of agreements, especially those relating to procedure.

It would be wrong to characterise these policies as 'neo-liberal'; to do so would be to endow them with an overall ideological coherence which they were never intended to possess. Nevertheless, they did spring from a deeply held conviction that the restoration of efficiency in British industry and society was much more likely to come about from greater incentives and more competition, rather than from incomes policies and economic planning—subjects upon which *Putting Britain Right Ahead* had very little to say (as commentators were quick to point out). We should also note that the new policies had been formulated without specific reference to the electoral appeal they were likely to have. The party did, at this time, embark upon an ambitious opinion-seeking exercise, using the services first of National Opinion Polls and later of Opinion Research Centre. The picture which emerged was of a party widely regarded as upper class, out of date, more competent at handling foreign policy than at steering the domestic ship of state, and badly tarnished by the events of

1961–4. These findings helped focus the collective mind of the party upon the need to establish a new image. But whether the new image, as represented by *Putting Britain Right Ahead*, was likely to result in an immediate rise in popularity was never convincingly demonstrated.

In 1966, given the choice between two parties each of which offered itself as manager of the mixed economy, the electorate preferred Labour under Harold Wilson. In opposition, prompted by the most controversial aspects of Labour government, the Conservatives revised and expanded the themes of their 1965 policy review, paying particular attention to three areas of policy that had major ideological implications. The first concerned incomes policies—specifically the implementation of statutory incomes policy under Labour from July 1966. The establishment of the National Board for Prices & Incomes, empowered to defer for investigation any proposed wage or price increase, seemed merely a more formal variation upon Conservative policy earlier in the decade. Heath, Macleod and Maudling were inclined—grudgingly—to support the proposal, or at least to acquiesce in it. But the 1922 Committee of backbench Conservative MPs had other ideas. Hitherto the most vocal source of Tory opposition to incomes policies had come from Enoch Powell. Now the parliamentary party declared itself overwhelmingly against the plan, partly out of conviction and partly because working-class opposition to a compulsory wages freeze threatened to become a major source of embarrassment for the Labour government.

This alliance of convenience between Conservative backbenchers and the working classes extended to one other area of public policy, namely immigration control and race relations. In the early 1950s the Conservatives had encouraged immigration, particularly from the Caribbean, as a way of coping with the post-war labour shortage in certain sectors (such as transport and nursing) while avoiding excessive wage increases. The Notting Hill 'race' riots of 1958 brought this policy to an end, and in 1962 the Macmillan government had legislated to bring Commonwealth immigration under systematic control—another sign that the idea of a global Empire, within which there was free movement of labour, was being abandoned.

In 1967 Enoch Powell and Duncan Sandys, a former Commonwealth Secretary, began agitating to stem the tide of Asian immigration from East Africa. These Asians had chosen to retain their British passports, and now, faced with ultra-nationalist regimes in Kenya and Uganda, demanded the right of entry into Britain that the passports were supposed to guarantee. The Labour government bowed to public pressure and legislated (1968) to impose an annual quota—a clear breach of promise which, however, the Conservative Shadow Cabinet supported. On 21 April 1968 Heath dismissed Powell from the Shadow Cabinet, a swift punishment following Powell's delivery, in Birmingham, of a brilliantly drafted speech warning of the dangers of racial strife if immigration were allowed to continue unchecked. Powell had said nothing that was not already party policy; the party had (admittedly with some notable dissentients) distanced itself from Labour's race-relations legislation (establishing a Community Relations Commission) and Heath had gone on record as wanting 'drastic' immigration control. Powell's crime was merely to have said publicly what many Tories thought privately, and to have proved himself the more popular Conservative spokesman. But though he was removed from the Shadow Cabinet the fact that trade unionists had marched to the House of Commons in his defence was very carefully noted: Powell was abandoned, but not the Powellite approach to immigration control.

The third area of policy to which the party paid particular attention at this time was that of taxation. *Putting Britain Right Ahead* envisaged a substantial reduction in direct taxation. This could only be brought about by reducing the scale of government activity, or by raising new indirect taxes. One by one the options open to a future Conservative government in the direction of reduced public spending were ruled out. Large-scale denationalisation, as advocated by the Powellites, was deemed beyond the realm of practical politics, and a reduction in the level of social services seemed likely to alienate electors, not attract them. The Conservative opposition could hardly call for less expenditure on defence when it was attacking the Labour government for pursuing just such a course. On the education front, Conservative policy at this time was to expand the system, not contract it, and (following the acceptance of the 1963 Robbins Report on Higher Education) to permit every school pupil with the necessary A-levels to proceed to university or technical college. A scheme to replace free education by giving parents education vouchers to spend (and top up) as they thought best was vetoed by the Conservative Research Department as politically disastrous.

Heath's answer to the problem of lowering direct taxation was not to reduce the level of government activity, but to undertake structural reforms that would yield, broadly speaking, the same amount of revenue, but in ways that would encourage private enterprise and initiative, not stifle them. Wide-ranging institutional reform, leading to greater efficiency, would enable government to uphold welfare benefits and social-service provision; reform of industrial relations and industrial training would make industry more efficient; taxation at the point of consumption, rather than at that of earnings, would give the government the revenue it needed while encouraging hard work.

It needs to be emphasised that this programme did not presuppose that there would be a total absence of reductions in public spending. Even before the 1966 election, proposals had been formulated (in *Putting Britain Right Ahead*) for the abolition of agricultural subsidies, and for the much more selective application of housing subsidies to the areas that were deemed to need them most. A 'war on waste' in government departments would (according to the 1966 Tory manifesto) lead to a saving of £400 million a year. But in the key areas of education, defence, pensions and the National Health Service no significant cuts were envisaged. 'It is an illusion [Macleod declared] to think that there are vast savings to be made . . . It is the tax system itself which is wrong and not the total tax burden.'[1] In short, new, indirect taxes had to be invented. Labour's Selective Employment Tax was, by now, yielding very large sums (£300 million in 1966–7, £600 million by 1970–1). Macleod was pledged to abolish it, but he was drawn by the notion of a Value-Added Tax (a form of taxation which the Common Market seemed likely to adopt) and by a 5 per cent payroll tax. In the event, the idea of a payroll tax was abandoned in the face of grass-roots constituency opposition to what was widely considered to be the continuation of Selective Employment Tax by another name. By 1969 Conservative opinion had gelled around the introduction of VAT, at a higher rate than originally anticipated, but with important exemptions, notably food.

Meanwhile, in a pamphlet—*Fair Deal At Work*—published in April 1968, the party unveiled its plans for trade-union reform: the legal enforcement of collective agreements; a new system of industrial courts; restrictions on sympathetic strikes, inter-union disputes and industrial actions designed to enforce the closed shop; protection for individual workers against closed-shop agreements; and the imposition of compulsory cooling-off periods and of secret ballots. Conservative spokesmen made it clear that the party was prepared to risk the confrontation with the unions that was bound to follow the enactment of such reforms. They pointed to the fact that public opinion, as reflected in opinion polls, was moving in favour of trade-union reform (which the Labour government was to attempt, unsuccessfully, to introduce in 1969). And they stressed that such reform would, in turn, be part of a much wider national modernisation programme aimed at introducing more rigorous management procedures into the public sector, setting ministries and public services policy goals and performance criteria. Some Conservatives, such as Nicholas Ridley and Sir Keith Joseph, wished to go further by cutting expenditure on nationalised industries and 'rolling back' the public sector. But the time was judged not yet ripe for official endorsement of such ideas.

In January 1970 the various separate strands of the policy review that had been under way over the past five years were brought together at a meeting of the Shadow Cabinet held at the Selsdon

Park Hotel, Croydon. The 'Selsdon Manifesto' contained, in itself, nothing new; on the question of taxation policy it was noticeably brief, not wishing to give hostages to fortune by proposing novel but unpopular methods of raising revenue. There was much emphasis on law-and-order, and on providing the requisite policing resources for its fulfilment. 'Selsdon Man' (the phrase was Harold Wilson's) looked forward to a much more competitive climate in the UK, and acknowledged that by reducing government subsidies to industry (for example, by phasing out the Regional Employment Premium), unemployment was bound to rise.

Admittedly, this was not quite the same approach as the deliberate use of unemployment to bring into being a less strident labour force. But the willingness to accept, more or less permanently, much higher levels of unemployment than had obtained in the 1950s and early 1960s, and the positive call for more selective social-security provision, clearly signalled the end of consensus politics. For the general election that took place a few months after the Selsdon meeting, Heath offered a manifesto—*A Better Tomorrow*—that drew heavily on the Selsdon approach: cuts in public expenditure; closer legal regulation of trade unions; contraction of the welfare state; harsh measures against 'shirkers and scroungers' who abused the social-security system; more prisons; stricter controls on immigration. In both content and tone the manifesto reads today like a prospectus for Thatcherite Conservatism. Some differences are evident, notably the reluctance of Heath and his colleagues to return already-nationalised industries to private ownership, and a commitment to 'increase the independence of local authorities' that clearly has no place in the Thatcherite approach. But the thrust of the 1970 manifesto, Heath's insistence that 'once a decision is made, once a policy is established, the Prime Minister and his colleagues should have the courage to stick to it', the avowed determination to offer a new style of government—these themes, reflecting as they did the views of a new generation of Conservatives and of a new generation of voters, verify and support Heath's claim to have effected a basic reorientation of Conservative politics.

The failure of Heath's government of June 1970–February 1974 to fulfil the promise of Selsdon had the profoundest repercussions upon the Conservative Party, acting as a motor for change in much the same way that the disappointments of Labour rule between 1974 and 1979 did in relation to the Labour left. The campaign in 1975 to have Heath replaced by Thatcher was based upon arguments that Heath's government (of which, of course, Mrs Thatcher and her champion, Sir Keith Joseph, had been prominent members) had merely tinkered with the old, Keynesian system of economic governance; that the ideal of a free-market economy had been negated by Heath's resort to incomes policies every bit as statutory as those of Wilson; that, far from taming the trade unions, Heath had allowed himself to be overawed and humiliated by them; and that public ownership and control of industry had been extended rather than curtailed. Above all, Heath's opponents within the party alleged that he had betrayed his own principles — enunciated in his Foreword to the 1970 manifesto — by demonstrating, time and again, that he lacked the will to govern. Under his leadership, it was argued, the Conservative Party had become heavily tarred by the brush of incompetence.

This is a damning indictment, and one, moreover, that is true as far as it goes. But like many political judgements it is based upon deliberately selective use of memory which it has been in the interests of Thatcherite Conservatives to foster and encourage for the past 15 years. Hindsight certainly enables us to understand what went wrong and why; but it must not be pressed into the service of party-political propaganda. Had Heath entered upon the premiership *after* and not before the Winter of Discontent, had he been appointed Prime Minister when year-on-year inflation was running at 18 per cent rather than at a relatively modest 8 per cent, and when unemployment stood at 1.5 million rather than at a mere 628,000, had he commenced his period of office knowing that public opinion was turning *against* public ownership, and not merely against *further* public ownership, the national mood would almost certainly have enabled him to do more.

In any case, in acknowledging the faults and failures of his administration we must also recognise his successes, his laying of the foundations upon which Thatcherite Britain has been constructed. To begin with, Heath presided over fundamental reform in the machinery of government. Businessmen were brought into the Civil Service Department to lend weight to the impetus for more efficient techniques of decision-making. This attack on the inertia of the Civil Service was further advanced by the establishment of the Central Policy Review Staff (CPRS), a body of academics, with Lord Rothschild at their head, attached to the Cabinet Office to give independent advice on policy issues. There was some streamlining of ministries by the creation of the Department of Trade & Industry and the Department of the Environment. There was a fundamental reform of local government, the first since 1888, resulting in a two-tier system of county councils and district councils; the antiquated institution of aldermen co-opted onto local authorities was abolished, and flat-rate attendance allowances for councillors were introduced. The 1972 Housing Finance Act cut subsidies to council-house tenants; local councils were urged to sell, to their tenants, the homes in which they lived. The 1973 Water Act, not without opposition from local councils, set up a system of Regional Water Authorities to manage water supply and sewage disposal.

The National Health Service Reorganisation Act, passed the same year at the behest of Sir Keith Joseph, established a network of 'managerial' Area Health Authorities to run a system whose bureaucracy had remained unchanged for nearly 30 years; one effect of this Act was, again, to reduce the role of elected local authorities in the social services. Most dramatically, it was the Heath government that took Britain into the Common Market, and which suffered all the political obloquy (not least from a section of the Conservative parliamentary party) which this bold decision entailed. The decisive 'Yes' vote in the 1975 referendum on continued membership of the EEC showed that Heath had public opinion behind him. Entry into the EEC was controversial when enacted in 1972; today those who condemn it are to be found largely on the margins of British political life.

To enumerate these achievements is not to deny the massive failures of which Heath's government was guilty. The economic dimensions of the Selsdon programme were implemented, but their implementation was quickly overtaken by unforeseen (but not, it must be said, unforeseeable) industrial problems. As proof positive of its determination to restore a free market in wage bargaining, the National Board for Prices & Incomes was abolished. But hopes of a voluntary agreement with the TUC and CBI quickly evaporated. In November 1972 a 90-day standstill on wages, salaries, rates, rents, dividends and prices (other than foods and imports) was imposed, and was followed (April 1973) by a Prices Commission and a Pay Board; in other words, a statutory pay policy had re-emerged.

Hopes of reducing the role of the state in industrial management were also dashed. There was some—very modest—hiving-off of state-run concerns, such as the Thomas Cook travel agency. Labour's Industrial Reorganisation Corporation was wound up, and the efforts of the nationalised gas industry in North Sea gas and oil exploration were curtailed. But the decision (February 1971) to take the aero-engine division of Rolls-Royce into public owner-ship was a clear breach of the promise that 'lame ducks' would not be rescued. The decision was eminently justifiable on grounds of public interest, since it was obviously undesirable that Britain should have to rely exclusively on foreign manufacturers of air-craft engines. In itself, the damage done to the government's credibility by this decision could probably have been limited. Unfortunately, it was not an isolated event. Later that year Upper Clyde Shipbuilders was rescued from liquidation. Worse was to follow in 1972, when the hapless Industry Minister, John Davies, announced his intention of introducing legislation (which became the 1972 Industry Act) giving the government powers of inter-vention in and financial assistance to industry so formidable that Tony Benn felt able to use them unamended as Davies's successor in Harold Wilson's last administration in 1974–5. 'I certainly am not nor ever have been', Davies told the Commons, 'an advocate of abandoning to their fate major sectors of British industry.'

The back of Selsdon Man had been well and truly broken. Why had this come about? To talk about a lack of will, or an absence of determination is to play into the hands of those, like the founders of the Selsdon Group (1973) whose charge that Heath was too much in love with collectivism ignored the fact that the decisions of which they complained had the backing of the Cabinet (and, therefore, of those in the Cabinet who were later to be identified with Mrs Thatcher's bid to oust Heath as leader). The key to an understanding of Heath's abandonment of Selsdon is to be found in his attitude, and in the attitude of his supporters in the party, to the ultra-sensitive issue of rising unemployment.

In private—and, very occasionally, in public—Conservatives had talked of the desirability of abandoning the consensus on full employment in order to bolster the competitiveness of industry by keeping wages as low as possible. While unemployment remained reasonably low—and, therefore, containable and (so it was argued) easily reversible—public opinion demanded that it be kept low, particularly in view of the fact that inflation was not yet a problem. Consequently, in the 1950s and 1960s, the popularity of governments had in truth been related to their degree of success in maintaining full employment. Once the wage-price spiral appeared to be out of control, the public's major concern was to bring inflation down; unemployment (which only reached the symbolic figure of one million in 1975) was a secondary consideration.

Only once, in 1972–3, did the Chancellor, Anthony Barber, deliberately attempt to reflate the economy; the major consideration of the 'Barber Boom' was to bring about faster economic growth, rather than to reduce unemployment. None the less, there can be no denying the fact that the Heath government was concerned to keep unemployment as low as possible. This was a price he was prepared to pay in order to gain the co-operation of the unions in the reform of industrial-relations law and in the implementation of effective wage-control policies.

Given the history of union opposition to Barbara Castle's attempted reform of industrial-relations law in 1969, and the well-known antipathy of the leadership of those unions to pay restraint, it is clear that Heath had no right to expect their co-operation, and no grounds for complaint (other than that of 'the nation in peril') when it was not forthcoming. Had he been a more ruthless man, he would have allowed unemployment to find its natural level, thus weakening the resolve of the trade-union movement to smash the 1971 Industrial Relations Act and to undermine his pay policy. But under Heath the Conservative Party still believed (in the words of its February 1974 election manifesto) in 'A Britain united in moderation, not divided by extremism'. That is, it was still a party in which the Disraelian hostility to 'Two Nations' had a special influence.

Conservatives do not easily forgive failures of leadership, and the party's defeat at both 1974 elections sealed the fate, not merely of Heath personally, but of the policies he had pursued of pay restraint (voluntary, according to the October 1974 manifesto) and wide-ranging dialogues with the trade unions. In October 1974 the manifesto had gone so far as to promise that even if the Conservatives won the election they would 'consult and confer with the leaders of other parties, and with the leaders of the great interests in the nation'; the possibility of a government of national unity was hinted at.

Heath's humiliation in the leadership election forced upon him by Tory backbenchers in February 1975 signalled the end of the One-Nation approach. Political commentators have often noted how much more ruthlessly the Conservative rank-and-file have dealt with unpopular leaders than has that of the Labour Party. The rejection of Heath was seen as a necessary step in the task of rebuilding the Conservative image. Edward Heath was therefore jettisoned (as Balfour had been in 1911) in the interests of the party's survival. Whoever succeeded him would be expected to project a very different image, even if many of the policies remained basically unchanged. But it was clear that these policies would now be targeted very firmly at those sections of the electorate capable of putting the Conservatives back in power. They would no longer have as their purpose the maintenance or achievement of any form of national consensus.

NOTE

1.   Quoted in D. Butler & M. Pinto-Duschinsky (1971), *The British General Election of 1970*, London, Macmillan, p. 72.

5. Thatcherism

In the previous chapter we saw how the consensual image of post-war Conservatism, as fashioned especially by Churchill and Macmillan, had been discarded in the late 1960s as a new generation of business-minded Tories had sought to equip the party with a sharper and much more distinctive set of policies. This programme went a considerable way towards sacrificing the sacred cows of post-war British society, especially the universality of the welfare state and the merit of state ownership of industry. It did not go so far as to question—officially—the desirability of maintaining full employment, and it was predicated, at least in part, on the necessity of affording the trade unions a central, consultative role in British government. The programme was also meant to inject new life into popular Toryism, by focusing upon those issues which, it seemed, agitated the British voting public, such as immigration control and law-and-order.

On the face of it, the Conservative defeats of 1974 might be said to have proved that the new programme—the declarations of Selsdon—had flopped; that the rejection of Heath implied also a rejection of the policies he had ostensibly tried to pursue. In fact, no such conclusion is justified, nor did Conservative policy-makers ever attempt such a justification. Heath lost the 1974 election contests not because the Selsdon programme had failed, but because the leader had shown himself incapable of carrying it through. The country entered upon a period of minority and near-minority Labour administrations, but no one with any political sense could argue that the nation had voted for socialism, for more state control, for greater freedoms for trade unions, or for more spending on the social services. The experiences of ever-quickening inflation, deeply unpopular compulsory incomes policies and unremitting industrial strife between 1974 and 1979 served only to bolster a public hostility to socialism that was already widespread, as the old 'smokestack' industries went into a final decline and, with them, an antiquated working class whose values a new generation of manual workers were clearly rejecting.

Heath lost in 1974, but only narrowly. His replacement by Thatcher should therefore be seen as a change of tactic, not a change of strategy. It is easy to forget now that in 1975 Mrs Thatcher was relatively unknown outside party circles. She had been in Parliament for less than 15 years, and had only held one Cabinet post, that of Education Secretary under Heath; the Education portfolio can be an important one, but it is not considered a Cabinet post of the first rank, merely a stepping stone to more prestigious jobs at the Exchequer or the Foreign Office. Mrs Thatcher was certainly not elected to the Tory leadership because she represented or had articulated any new set of beliefs; she, together with the two strongest contenders for the job, Keith Joseph and William Whitelaw (the Deputy Leader), had been members of the Heath government and party to all its sins and misdemeanours.

Mrs Thatcher's election to the leadership is explained by reference to three factors: first, as a woman her candidature had a certain novelty about it, which was bound to draw the attention of the media in a positive way; second, in the first leadership ballot (4 February 1975) none of Heath's closest colleagues had the guts to stand against him, only the enigmatic backbencher Sir Hugh Fraser (whose 16 votes deprived Mrs Thatcher of the majority she needed, so necessitating a second ballot the following week); third, Margaret Thatcher was, in terms of personality and style, as unlike Heath as could possibly be imagined. Though their backgrounds were in some ways remarkably similar (lower-middle-class, grammar-school and Oxford-educated), Mrs Thatcher had about her an earnestness and a forthrightness, a moral fervour and an avowed concern for family values which Heath may well have shared to the full, but which he was never able to project publicly.

There is much truth in the view that Mrs Thatcher was elected because she was not Mr Heath. Equally, however, we must guard against accepting the idea that she was elected because she represented some new intellectual doctrine such as 'monetarism'. Monetarism may be defined as the belief that inflation is caused by an excessive amount of money in the economy and that, therefore, the cure for inflation lies in controlling the money supply through devices such as high interest rates (to restrict private credit) and strict limits on government borrowing. The corollary of this view is that the government should intervene to bring about such monetary control—and, indeed, that it is the government rather than, say, the trade unions, which is responsible for the inflation to be found in the economy.

Monetarism in its British guise was not, as a matter of historical fact, an invention of Thatcherite political economy. There are, indeed, strong grounds for looking upon the deflationary package introduced by Callaghan's Labour government in 1976 (as a condition of the granting of an unprecedented IMF loan facility of $3.9 billion) as the true triumph of monetarist principles; Callaghan's speech at the September 1976 Labour Party Conference at Blackpool, with its denunciation of Keynesian policies, its condemnation of the idea that governments could spend their way out of recession, and its plea to 'get back to fundamentals' represented the authoritative—if reluctant—voice of monetarism in the raw. It has often been quoted back at the Labour Party by Thatcherite Conservatives. But it is not what Thatcherism is all about.

The classic doctrine of monetarism exonerates trade unions from blame for inflation, because monetarists deny that inflation stems from excessive wage demands. Thatcherism sees trade unions as having played a central part in Britain's relative economic decline in the twentieth century, through their resistance to rationalisation and modernisation of shop-floor practices (so hindering and sometimes crippling efforts to raise productivity) and through their pursuit of unrealistic wage levels (so causing unemployment and falling standards of living, both of which lead—it is said—to calls for the money supply to be expanded so as to reflate the economy). Monetarists would deny the trade unions a say in the formulation of economic policy, but only because in the world of monetarism the unions are worthy of neither praise nor blame for the state of the economy; they are merely guilty of doing what comes naturally to them. Thatcherism denies the unions an effective voice because trade unionism, certainly as it has existed in Britain since the First World War, is seen as an unmitigated evil—and (worse still) an unmitigated *socialist* evil—an unnatural growth that must be isolated and neutralised.

A relentless assault upon the power of trade unions has been a central feature of Mrs Thatcher's economic policy, and she has shown herself to be impatient with those, such as James Prior (Employment Secretary 1979–81) who have urged a cautious approach to trade-union reform. Prior's Employment Act of 1980 did no more than bestow upon employers the right to take legal action against secondary picketing, and limited the introduction of new 'closed shop' agreements to cases where 80 per cent of union members, voting in a secret ballot, approved such arrangements. At the same time public funds were made available to finance such ballots, and those who were deemed to have been unreasonably excluded or expelled from a union because of the operation of a closed shop were given a right to compensation.

Prior's successor, Norman Tebbit (1981–3) went much further in his 1982 Employment Act by restricting the operation of existing closed shops to cases where a majority of union members, voting in secret ballots, approved such arrangements, giving employers further legal remedies against secondary industrial action, and by making trade unions (rather than individual trade unionists) liable for damages in respect of industrial actions deemed by the courts to be unlawful. Tom King's Trade Union Act of 1984 stipulates that exemption from civil actions for damages can only arise if industrial action has been preceded by a secret ballot of union members. The 1988 Employment Act has removed entirely the legal immunity previously enjoyed by unions taking action to enforce a closed shop.

By stages, therefore, the clock has been turned back almost to the situation that existed at the very beginning of the century. Industrial disputes have been in large measure transformed into law-and-order issues. A union that initiates a dispute in a manner which a High Court judge deems to be unlawful risks civil action for damages, fines for contempt of court and—ultimately— sequestration of its assets. The internal democracy of the unions has certainly been strengthened by the imposition of secret ballots; in this sense Mrs Thatcher is justified in claiming that under the Conservatives the unions have been handed back to their members. But this reform of the machinery of union decision-making has been nothing more than a preliminary to the deliberate undermining of union authority. In its 1987 manifesto the party boasted that its trade-union reforms had prevented 'coercion of the majority by activists and militants'. But its 1988 legislation, protecting individual union members from disciplinary action should they refuse to join a strike fairly called after a secret ballot, demonstrates a rather different preoccupation.

Once again, we can exonerate the Thatcherites from any originality in drafting the blueprint upon which this policy is based; they have taken up (admittedly, with a determination not shown by politicians hitherto) where the 1971 Industrial Relations Act left off, and much of that legislation had in any case been foreshadowed by the ill-fated Labour White Paper of 1969. But whereas Labour in 1969 and the Conservatives in 1971 were concerned only to reform *industrial relations*, the Thatcher government has, by stages, revealed that it has a very different end in view. The aim is not to democratise the unions, but to destroy them in their existing form, by transforming them into glorified friendly societies, offering a range of services (such as private health insurance) to their members and acting for them in a purely consultative role in bargaining on pay and conditions, but quite unable to confront employers and prevail over them in industrial disputes.

Thatcherism does not see industrial trade unions as part of the natural economic order. Rather, it views them as acting 'in restraint of trade', much as the political economists of the late eighteenth and early nineteenth centuries regarded them. To anyone with a smattering of knowledge of Disraelian Conservatism it will be apparent at once that the Thatcherite view is Liberal rather than Conservative and that, as we noted in the previous chapter, it reflects that branch of Conservative thinking that blossomed only after the entry into the party of the bourgeois refugees from the Liberal Party that split in 1886. The label of Conservatism has been put on a bottle whose contents amount to nothing less than a full-bloodied Liberal political economy.

New Conservatism is but old Liberalism writ large. Its central feature is what Professor Andrew Gamble terms 'the social market economy',[1] and its influence can be traced back to the writings of Adam Smith (1723–90), Jeremy Bentham (1748–1832) and other founding-fathers of nineteenth-century economic *laissez-faire*. Until her elevation to the Tory leadership Mrs Thatcher had never evinced much interest in economic theory. From her father, the self-made grocer, Methodist and Independent mayor of Grantham, she learned the virtues of thrift and hard work. But it was from the Jews of Finchley (the only constituency she has ever represented in Parliament) that she learned how people can, apparently by their own efforts and without the assistance of the state, triumph against every kind of adversity. And it was the Jew Sir Keith Joseph who introduced her to social market economics and, in particular, to the writings of Friedrich von Hayek and Milton Friedman. If Thatcherism has any intellectual coherence, it is to be found in the reformulation of these views by Joseph and his associates, in particular Sir Alfred Sherman, another Jew, who became Joseph's speech-writer and Director of his Centre for Policy Studies, which was established in 1974 with Mrs Thatcher as its President.

During the 1970s several different pressures exerted a collective force on the Conservative Party, pushing it in a direction—that of the free market—in which its membership, untroubled by memories of the 1930s and by the guilt associated with the deprivation of that decade, were only too eager to go. Enoch Powell has some claim to have re-introduced Conservatives to the virtues of the free market. His attacks on prices and incomes policies ('a dangerous nonsense') were brilliantly executed, but his descent into the politics of racial prejudice, even though applauded by many in the party, put him beyond the pale. By contrast, the work of the Austrian intellectual Hayek and of the American economist Friedman conferred first-rate intellectual respectability.

In a slim volume—*The Road To Serfdom*—published in London in 1944, Hayek condemned the notion of central planning (which Stalin's Russia had espoused and the virtues of which had captivated British socialists) as destructive of liberty on two levels: central planning required, in practice, an increasingly authoritarian state, with power draining from the legislature (Parliament) to the executive (Whitehall); moreover, central planning destroyed competition and led inevitably to the establishment of state monopolies which, in turn, would stifle innovation and breed inefficiency. In an attack not merely on socialists but on Keynesians and on those, like Macmillan, who sought a compromise between overall planning and total freedom, Hayek extolled the social virtues of the spontaneous market. In the operation of this market the state has but one role, to ensure that the market operates indiscriminately. Its obligation to provide welfare services exists only as long as these do no more than guarantee a minimum level of subsistence. Beyond that, all policies aimed at redistributing resources are condemned. Hayek's society will, by his own admission, be full of arbitrary inequalities. This is the price that must be paid for economic liberty, upon which he places an incomparably higher value.

Two further features of Hayek's work, governed as it must be by a concept reminiscent of social Darwinism (the survival of the fittest), are worthy of mention here, in the context of Conservative rule in Britain since 1979. The first (developed by Hayek in his later writings) is that strong trade unions, no less than interventionist governments, are destructive of liberty, because their activities constitute an unnatural influence upon the operation of the market. The second concerns the relationship between economic liberty and political democracy. In a truly democratic society, in which the rights of minorities are respected but, otherwise, the view of the majority prevails, it is more than likely that irresistible pressures will arise for central intervention, and that (especially where economic and social resources have come to be concentrated in the hands of a few) demands will be made for state action to redistribute wealth and curb market excesses; in short, the operation of the social market will be challenged by the purveyors of social democracy, articulating the claims of the community against those of the individual.

Hayek recognised that the workings of the democratic state could easily destroy the society he envisaged and, for that reason, he was understandably critical of it. In *The Political Order of a Free People* (1979) he noted that 'Britain gave the world . . . the pernicious principle of parliamentary sovereignty', and he condemned 'what today we call democratic government' on the grounds that such government amounted to nothing more than 'the varied interests of a conglomerate of pressure groups whose support the government must buy by the grant of special benefits'. Government, in Hayek's view, must be free to govern irrespective of the wishes of the people because 'the basic principle of a free society [is] that the coercive powers of government are restricted to the enforcement of universal rules of just conduct, and cannot be used for the achievement of particular purposes'. 'I am fairly certain [he wrote] that the days of unlimited democracy are numbered.'

Tragically, therefore, in condemning one road to serfdom, Hayek actually pointed the way to another.[2] Conservative proponents of the social market economy are less troubled on this account because, under the first-past-the-post electoral system, true majoritarian rule is most unlikely to come about. The Thatcherite governments that have ruled Britain since 1979 have been minority governments, against which the threat of a backlash by a theoretical majority (especially in a multi-party situation) has, in practice, been negligible. British 'democracy' has, therefore, provided an ideal test-tube in which to stir Professor Hayek's lethal mixture.

The latent totalitarianism of Hayek's political economy has been moderated by the social thought of Milton Friedman, a monetarist guru whose major influence on Conservative thought has been to stress the positive and liberal aspects of a relatively unfettered capitalist economic system. Friedman (whose parents were petty-bourgeois Jewish immigrants to the USA from central Europe) has provided definitive blueprints for the creation of a monetarist economy; but he has also stressed the personal freedoms that would, in his view, flow from such a society. Thus, the abolition of rent controls, of subsidies to manufacturing industries and of minimum-wage and other employment legislation would have a positive aspect: the creation of a social system in which there would be much greater freedom of choice, even for the very poor, who would receive cash benefits rather than payments in kind and free social services.

Friedman has also espoused the idea of education vouchers, given to parents to spend on their children's education as they think fit—a policy which is likely to result in the growth of private-sector education. Like many Americans who reacted against the 'welfarism' of 'big government' as practised by successive Democratic administrations, Friedman has argued in favour of legislative action to prevent deficit budgeting and excessive public spending. Whilst this idea, baldly stated, has not found favour with Mrs Thatcher's governments, it has permeated the Thatcherite state in other ways, through such devices as the imposition of cash limits on departments of government and the statutory restriction of local-government spending.

In immediate post-war Britain the views of Friedman, Hayek and their followers were distinctly unfashionable. They were, however, kept alive through the activities of a series of pressure groups, of whom the most influential was the Institute of Economic Affairs (IEA), established in London in 1956 by the businessman Anthony Fisher. For more than a quarter of a century the IEA has acted as the principal disseminator of anti-Keynesian propaganda, aiming its publications not at a mass audience but at a carefully selected group of opinion-formers and decision-makers. One of its most significant contributions to the creation of a specifically British form of social-market economics has been through the publicity it has given to critiques of government-run monopolies, which (it is argued) are unresponsive to market forces and which deny consumer choice. Its publications have included demands for more competition in the provision of health and education services, an end to exchange controls, the breaking-up and privatisation of publicly owned enterprises, the sale of council houses and more scope for the private provision of pensions; all these policies have found their way into the legislative programme of the Thatcher governments.

In the 1960s the exhortations of the IEA fell on distinctly stony ground. But in the 1970s its work began to bear fruit. Politicians of the calibre of Sir Keith Joseph and Sir Geoffrey Howe paid court to it, and its ideas began to be reflected in the leader columns of *The Times* and in the writings of a new generation of academic economists. These ideas have also spawned and encouraged other anti-consensual pressure groups, notably the Centre for Policy Studies (1974), the National Association for Freedom (1975), the Adam Smith Institute (1977) and the Social Affairs Unit (1980). These groups have all had immediate and less immediate aims.

The Social Affairs Unit has directed its attention towards the formulation of an alternative to Beveridge-inspired social policy; its ethos, in other words, is anti-welfare state, and it delights in undermining the wisdom received from social do-gooders and left-wing sociologists. One of the Unit's prime targets has been the Church of England; in recent years it has taken especial pleasure in undermining the social gospel of Archbishop Runcie of Canterbury, as reflected in the Report of his Commission on *Faith in the City*. The Adam Smith Institute has concentrated its attack on the erosion of personal liberty and on the intrusion of the public sector into people's lives, particularly over economic affairs and local government. The National Association for Freedom campaigns for the rights of private enterprise and the need to protect personal liberties from the predatory instincts of the trade-union movement.

But a wider set of purposes is common to all these organisations: they have all set out to restrict the power of central government, no matter in what direction their particular interest has taken them;

and they have all concentrated their fire-power on the Conservative Party, or elements thereof. The establishment of the Centre for Policy Studies marked a more formal approach to the attainment of this objective: the conversion of the party to social-market economics. The CPS was set up deliberately to act as a counterweight to the Conservative Research Department, which in 1974 was still heavily influenced by the consensus politics of the generations of Macmillan and Butler. Following the Conservative defeat of February 1974 Sir Keith Joseph conducted a series of measured attacks on the financial and industrial policies of the Heath government. In August the CPS was established. On 5 September, in a speech at Preston, Joseph (who had refused to serve in Heath's Shadow Cabinet) repudiated Keynesian demand-management and other devices that had been used by governments since 1945 to regulate the economy—including, of course, incomes policies; in its place he called for a monetarist approach to conquering inflation, and proclaimed himself ready to accept 'action which might threaten some jobs' in order to see this policy through to a successful conclusion.

At the time the Preston speech caused fury and dismay in Conservative ranks. Another general election was imminent; the speech was reckoned to have handed Labour a propaganda victory. But in the Conservative leadership battle some months later (and with the *next* general election now clearly some years away), Joseph's critique of the Heath government carried more weight. With Mrs Thatcher firmly in place, the deliberations and publications of the CPS and other 'New Right' pressure groups provided her with a selection of ready-made policies, a constant underlying theme of which was the evil that flowed from the power of central government. From the argument that the economy needed to be liberated so that market forces might operate unchecked, and from the belief that a wasteful and inefficient public sector needed to be drastically pruned, it was but a short step to the view that people generally in Britain had come to expect too much of government, and had, indeed, been pampered by it. A return to self-reliance and self-help (both virtues purveyed by Gladstonian Liberalism) was deemed to be long overdue. The entire 1979 Conservative manifesto was predicated on the view that the power of the state had grown, was growing, and ought to be diminshed so as to restore 'the enterprise and effort on which a prosperous country . . . depends'.

That the policies pursued by the Thatcher administrations since 1979 have amounted to anything but a return to limited (or 'small') government will become obvious when we examine the policies and their impact in detail. Thatcherism in practice has meant a very substantial, and in some respects frightening, increase in the power of the state: rights have been curtailed and freedoms have been constricted. To understand how such a paradoxical situation has come about we need to remember that the outpourings of the New Right in the 1970s were not aimed at the mass electorate, nor did they amount to a co-ordinated attempt to construct an alternative to social democracy. Rather, they reflected the views of a wide variety of thinkers, politicians and industrialists, sometimes doing little more than disguising personal or institutional prejudices as political beliefs. In any case, the Conservative victory of 1979 was due, as much as anything else, to a national weariness with a weak, minority administration that seemed incapable of governing. In 1979 those sections of the electorate that did not vote Labour wanted strong government; as a politician Mrs Thatcher recognised the force of this argument.

Mrs Thatcher has borrowed freely from the New Right when it has suited her so to do; but she has not slavishly followed every one of its prescriptions to the letter. Her policies have also been influenced by a different, and more sinister, Conservative outlook, to which the term 'New Right' has been applied either out of confusion or simply in order to make mischief. This outlook is frankly authoritarian; the *Salisbury Review*, edited by Professor Roger Scruton, is its acknowledged mouthpiece, and its adherents and propagators include the Cambridge dons Maurice Cowling and Edward Norman, and the editor of the *Sunday Telegraph*, Peregrine Worsthorne. Professing a quite proper concern with permissiveness and declining moral values, this group draw spiritual comfort from the writings and speeches of Immanuel Jakobovits, the Chief Rabbi of the United Synagogue whom Mrs Thatcher promoted to the House of Lords in 1988. The forthright condemnations which Jakobovits has made over the years of sexual licence and lack of a sense of personal discipline (not merely in sexual matters but also in the social and economic spheres) echo perfectly the sentiments of the Prime Minister in relation to family values; and she has clearly been attracted by Worsthorne's plea for the authority of the state to be re-activated so as to counteract 'libertarian mish-mash'.[3]

In this way certain themes which are anything but new to Conservatism have come to the surface once more, the boldness of those who proclaim them bolstered by the thought that (as in times past) they can be made to possess a certain popular appeal. These themes include a repudiation of feminist culture; an attack on homosexuality; a preoccupation with national identity; an aversion to non-white immigration; a suspicion of civil liberties; and an obsession with law-and-order. Mrs Thatcher's personal liking for them, and her determination to exploit them for political advantage, were evident even before she became Prime Minister. In October 1977 she confessed to the party Conference:

People have asked me whether I am going to make the fight

against crime an issue at the next election. No, I am not going to make it an issue. It is the people of Britain who are going to make it an issue.

There was of course no doubt that many people felt agitated and uneasy by rising crime statistics, especially relating to crimes of violence; about three-quarters of the electorate told pollsters in 1979 that they favoured a return of the death penalty for murder, a policy which Mrs Thatcher personally supported. However, the 1979 manifesto commitment to a free vote in the House of Commons on hanging amounted to no more than a promise to let the Commons express a view; the restoration of the death penalty was rejected (July 1979) by a majority of 119, and has continued to be rejected by large majorities ever since.

Under Mrs Thatcher, in fact, the restoration of the death penalty has never been Conservative policy. The promise to introduce tougher sentences for young offenders—the 'short sharp shock'—merely allowed an experiment to get under way; the experiment was not a success. The notorious 'sus' law (part of the 1824 Vagrancy Act), permitting convictions on mere suspicion of intent, was repealed and replaced by the 1981 Criminal Attempts Act; and the Police & Criminal Evidence Act of the same year gave the law-enforcement agencies new powers of detention and investigation—balanced, however, by new rights for those under arrest. The 1982 Criminal Justice Act introduced greater flexibility in sentencing; but successive Tory Home Secretaries have urged non-custodial sentences wherever possible, in order to reduce gross overcrowding in the prison system—in itself an admission that the law-and-order 'problem' has not yet been solved.

Thatcherite policy on law-and-order has, therefore, consisted of a great deal of rhetoric, skilfully aimed, but little reality. The most draconian initiative in this field came in 1988, with the making permanent of the 1976 Prevention of Terrorism Act; since this was a Labour measure, the Conservatives are hardly in a position to take credit for it. In one respect, however, Thatcherism has taken substantive action, in the general direction of 'law-and-order', in order to redeem election promises. Long before Mrs Thatcher had been thought of as a potential leader, the Conservatives had seen in the issue of immigration a vote-winner. In a television interview in January 1978 Mrs Thatcher talked about the need to quell the fears of 'people . . . [who] . . . feel rather swamped' by coloured immigrants; the theme was pressed home by Sir Keith Joseph during the Ilford North by-election the following March. The Labour government rejected the advice of an all-party select committee (April) that stricter controls on the entry of immigrants be introduced. But the Conservatives took up the cry, and in 1979 promised the electors a series of measures designed to achieve very substantial reductions in the numbers of immigrants allowed in from the New Commonwealth and Pakistan (NCWP).

Whilst some of these proposals (such as the much-vaunted finite register of dependants) had to be abandoned on technical grounds, there can be little doubt that the reduction of the rate of NCWP immigration (from 37,000 in 1979 to 30,300 in 1982) was an achievement of sorts. It was accompanied by a Nationality Act (1981) which defined the right of abode in Britain in such a way as to uncouple it, for the first time, from the fact of birth in Britain. In practice, only those whites with close ties to the mother country now have an automatic right of entry to and settlement in Britain, while the ability of non-whites already settled here (especially those originating from India and Pakistan) to bring in foreign-born spouses has been severely curtailed. Interestingly, when an earlier policy, to allow men settled in the UK to bring in and marry foreign wives, but not vice-versa, was condemned as sexually discriminatory by the European Court of Human Rights, the reaction of the Thatcher government was to tighten the law to exclude both wives and husbands rather than to extend to women the right already enjoyed by men. Interestingly, too, the Conservative government which pleaded that its tough immigration laws were necessary to ensure good race relations and prevent overcrowding had no qualms about allowing into Britain some 10,000 refugees from Communism in Vietnam.

The pursuit of racially motivated and sexist objectives has entailed a growth of the power of the state; this has been generally portrayed as government in the national interest, and its application has extended into many other spheres. In 1987, for example, the right of MPs to make representations on behalf of persons facing deportation was deliberately curtailed. The freedom of those who work at the Government Communications Headquarters at Cheltenham to belong to trade unions has been abolished (January 1984). The right of schoolteachers to belong to unions has been preserved, but the right of these unions to negotiate pay and conditions on behalf of their members has been overridden. The party which historically has supported the sanctity of contracts has legislated (1988) to deprive university teachers of their contractual rights. The government has resorted increasingly to injunctions to prevent newspapers, radio and television from making public material which it considers sensitive. Its attempts to prevent people in Britain from reading the memoirs of the former secret agent Peter Wright (*Spycatcher*)— even though these memoirs were freely available abroad—have earned it world-wide notoriety. The Broadcasting Standards Council, established in 1988 in fulfilment of a 1987 manifesto promise, may well become a tool of real censorship, in that the request made by its chairman, Lord Rees-Mogg, that it be allowed to preview programmes, could easily be used to prevent them from being shown.

In no respect, however, has the extension of the authority of the state under Thatcherite Conservatism been more dramatic, or more systematic, than in the destruction of local government. The development is all the more startling, and demonstrates all the more dramatically the divergence between Thatcherism and consensus Conservatism, when we recall the support for autonomous local government given by previous Conservative administrations: the establishment of county councils (1888) and of the London boroughs (1899), the Education Acts of 1902 and 1944, the London Government Act of 1963 (establishing the GLC in place of the LCC) and the Local Government Act of 1972 (establishing six metropolitan and 47 non-metropolitan counties in England and Wales), not to mention the support given by Conservative governments between the wars (notably by Neville Chamberlain's 1923 Housing Act) to the policy of Treasury subsidy of local-authority house-building.

The Thatcherite assault upon local government has sprung from two sources. The first has arisen as an inevitable result of the adoption of a monetarist approach to the control of inflation. By 1980 roughly 63 per cent of local-authority expenditure was derived from the national Exchequer; in order to control public spending it was therefore deemed necessary to control spending by town-halls and county-halls, not merely of the Treasury element but of the total budgets of the local-government sector. Local-government expenditure had (it was argued) to be contained within set targets, or limits. These broad aims were incorporated into the Local Government Acts of 1980 and 1982; the 1982 legislation also established an Audit Commission, with powers to examine the efficiency and effectiveness of local services and to surcharge local councillors deemed to have acted irresponsibly or illegally in setting rates and authorising local expenditure. Local councillors can now find themselves being asked to explain to a non-elected District Auditor how and why they voted at particular council meetings; a reply to the effect that they voted in line with local-election commitments and promises made to their constituents is unlikely to afford them much protection. The 1988 Local Government Act has taken this intrusion into the relationship between electors and councillors a stage further, by giving the Auditor the power to issue a prohibition order, preventing a council from doing what the Auditor *believes* to be illegal—whether the proposed action is illegal or not.

The justification for these measures lay primarily within the view that central government had always had an implicit right to control local spending, that this right existed even if it had never before been enshrined in legislation, and that this 'implicit consensus' had broken down largely due to the irresponsibility of some local authorities in not recognising, in their spending policies, central government's authority and supremacy in such matters. The Conservatives therefore replaced a system by which Exchequer support had been related to past expenditure (high spending authorities received more central grant) by one in which, broadly speaking, the rate of government grant was progressively reduced once a council's spending rose above a limit pre-set in Whitehall. When some local authorities (mainly but not exclusively Labour-controlled) sought to compensate for this belt-tightening by raising extra revenue from the rates, the only source of finance then under their own control, the Conservative response was to legislate (1984) so as to require local authorities to set rates within limits determined by the government.

At first glance 'rate-capping' seems justified, or at least justifiable, on the monetarist principle. A subsidiary but none the less important argument was that business ratepayers were being heavily burdened by high-spending authorities in whose election they played no part; so far as business and commercial ratepayers were concerned, this really did seem to be a case of taxation without representation. But on closer examination the argument turns out to be spurious. In the nineteenth century, when the right to vote in national as well as local elections was determined by a property qualification, the virtual disfranchisement of business ratepayers would have been unthinkable. But in 1918 the right to vote was detached from the possession of property, and in 1948 the business vote at parliamentary elections was abolished. Residence, not wealth, now determines whether or not a citizen has a vote, and that vote is a personal, not a corporate, privilege. It would of course have been possible for the Conservatives to have restored the business vote in 1984—and, indeed, to have gone further, by giving both personal and corporate votes in proportion to rateable values of property occupied: the more rates that were paid, the more votes that could be cast; but even Patrick Jenkin, the Environment Secretary, ruled this out as totally regressive.

Rate-capping dealt with a major complaint of the business ratepayers, and satisfied Treasury demands for much tighter control of local-authority spending. It also went some way to meeting the second principal Thatcherite objective in the field of local-government reform, namely to deprive Labour voters of the opportunity to pursue, in the arena of local government, policies of which central government disapproved. The relative freedom enjoyed by local government before 1980 made it possible for Labour local authorities to mitigate some of the effects of Conservative rule. Most Labour councils, for instance, were luke-warm towards the sale of council houses to their tenants, and some were frankly obstructionist, claiming—rightly—that those who had voted them into office disapproved of this policy. The Housing Acts of 1980 and 1984 forced such authorities to toe the government's line; at the same time the ability of local councils to subsidise rents through the rates was heavily curtailed, even though the Treasury continues to subsidise the mortgages of home-buyers through tax relief. In 1988 Environment Secretary Nicholas Ridley announced that the government intended in future to control the amounts local authorities borrow, so as to block 'leaseback' arrangements by means of which government-imposed spending restrictions were being circumvented; Ridley also promised that he would take powers to force local councils to use empty council-houses.

Other Conservative complaints against Labour-controlled local authorities centred around the determination of some councils to pursue foreign-policy initiatives, and otherwise to engage in political posturing that ran counter to Thatcherite values. In the capital the Greater London Council, under left-wing Labour control from 1981, subsidised pro-Palestinian pressure groups, welcomed Irish Nationalists and set up a police monitoring unit; many Labour-run councils adopted toward the police an attitude that can be best summarised as malevolently neutral, restricting (for example) the access of local police forces to schools while extending patronage to organisations perceived as hostile to police interests. Attempts to present a so-called 'balanced' view of homosexuality in schools were perceived by many (not just within the Tory Party) as assaults upon family values.

The Education Act of 1986 and the Local Government Act of 1988 have placed severe restrictions upon the ability of any local authority to use ratepayers' money in the pursuit of political objectives; the right of police access to schools has been guaranteed, while the promotion of homosexuality has, to all intents and purposes, been forbidden. The boycotting, by local authorities, of goods from countries (such as South Africa) whose policies they oppose is now illegal; local councillors cannot (Lord Bellwin told the House of Lords on 28 January 1988) meddle 'in national matters that were not their concern'. In these ways the rights of local electors have been so hedged about as to be, now, virtually not worth exercising. The problem of Labour control of the six Metropolitan Counties (all in the north of England) and of the GLC and the Inner London Education Authority has been solved by the simple expedient of legislating these bodies out of existence. We are left with a system of district councils, London borough councils, county councils and Scottish regional councils whose major tasks are simply to act as local arms of the central government; the freedom given to state schools in the 1988 Education Act to opt out of local-authority control, and become directly funded by the state, promises to constrict further the area of local initiative.

The attempts of Mrs Thatcher's administrations to control local-authority expenditure have not been an unqualified success. As a proportion of total public spending, local-government capital expenditure has fallen sharply (mainly because of the contraction of new housebuilding programmes), but local-authority *current* spending has risen, both in absolute terms and in relation to total public spending. In the early 1980s spokesmen across the political spectrum acknowledged the anomalies and inequities of the system of raising local revenue via the rates. In this respect too, however, the opportunity to effect a much-needed reform has been compromised by narrower political aims. The major weakness of the rating system is that it is unrelated to the ability to pay. In Scotland the Conservative policy of replacing rates by a community charge was, by common consent, a major source of anti-government feeling during the 1987 election; the extension of this policy to the rest of the country was the occasion (18 April 1988) for the biggest revolt of Tory backbenchers under Mrs Thatcher.

The institution of a flat-rate community charge has brought together some of the underlying themes of Thatcherite Conservatism. First, it has a wholly disproportionate impact upon the poor, most of whom will have to pay something and many of whom will have to pay the charge in full; this, it is argued, will help instil into them a sense a responsibility for the financial policies of those whom they elect to office in the town- and county-halls. Secondly, in its operation it represents the exact opposite of 'soaking the rich'. Those who live in a 'twelve up, twelve down' mansion will pay no more than those living in a 'two up, two down' terraced dwelling in the same local-authority area; the principle of One Nation is thus deemed to have been upheld. Thirdly, industry and commerce will no longer be at the mercy of local authorities, because they will pay the community charge at a standard ('unified') business rate set by the government; the business world is thus protected from the democracy of the town-hall.

Finally, the institution of a community charge has the merit of appearing to restore local accountability. Rates were not paid by everyone; many citizens had, therefore, no qualms about voting for local councillors with high spending policies, for these citizens knew they would not carry much, if any, of the consequent financial burden. Almost everyone will pay some community charge, and most will pay it in full; citizens who want their local authority to give a high level of service are at liberty to vote the appropriate party into office, but will have to live with the financial consequences thereof.

This new regime, in redemption of the 1987 election promise to 'reform local government finance to strengthen local democracy and accountability', is in fact seriously flawed, because the government has retained its power to 'cap' community charges that it (rather than local electors) feels are excessive. The declaration incorporated into the 1987 Conservative manifesto that 'Local electors must be able to decide the level of service they want and how much they are prepared to pay for it' is, in this respect, so superficial and qualified as to be largely devoid of real meaning. And the intention to 'require' local authorities to put out to tender a range of services, including refuse collection, the cleaning of streets and buildings, and catering reflects the contempt in which the wishes of local electorates are really held.

The destruction of local democracy must surely rank as one of the most dramatic and far-reaching achievements of Conservative rule since 1979—a break not merely with the post-war consensus, but with a much earlier consensus at least 100 years old. Local government used to be run by Lords Lieutenant and magistrates appointed by the Crown; in 1989 the chains in which elected local authorities have been bound have turned them back into agents of Whitehall.

This return to Victorian (or, more correctly, pre-Victorian) values has been mirrored by the Thatcherite attitude towards the welfare state. In the context of the much wider aim to reduce government spending and taxation, the concept of an all-embracing welfare state, providing a reasonable level of social security for all, 'from the cradle to the grave', was bound to suffer. Indeed, it is fair to add that attempts to contain overall expenditure on the social and health services pre-dated the Thatcher governments. From 1975 to 1978 the Labour government reduced spending on housing and education, and managed (through cash limits) to contain increases in the cost of personal social services and social security; between 1975 and 1977 total spending on the social services (social security, the National Health Service, employment services, personal social services, housing and education) fell by 0.4 per cent.[4] Thereafter there was a modest rise (of the order of about 1 per cent) during the remainder of Labour's period of office. Overall, under Labour housing expenditure suffered a reduction of 13 per cent and spending on education fell by 6 per cent.

These trends represent the outcomes of deliberate policy choices, and undoubtedly give ammunition to those who argue that the attack on the welfare state began under Labour. What needs to be stressed is that it was never part of Labour policy permanently to deprive the welfare state of the resources it required. The cuts were forced on the Labour government by economic circumstances, and were not applied across the board; spending on personal social services, for example, grew, under Labour, by about 8 per cent. Socialists were quick to criticise the cuts as regressive and degenerate; but the charge that the welfare state was being starved of resources in order to facilitate its dismantling was never seriously brought. Under Thatcher, a quite different set of philosophies has been put into operation, with the result that the maintenance of a welfare state has been subordinated to other objectives declared to be much more fundamental to the national interest.

Given the commitments to cut public spending, reduce the public-sector borrowing requirement and shift from direct to indirect taxation, a real and substantial reduction in government spending on the welfare services has inevitably been sought. But it has not been easy to achieve. As the recession deepened in the early 1980s, rising unemployment put extra burdens on welfare services; social-security payments rose. In addition, the growing number of people living beyond retirement age claimed state pensions and, very often, other welfare payments. Between 1979 and 1983, for example, the number of registered unemployed persons rose from 1.3 million (5 per cent of the workforce) to 3.0 million (over 12 per cent); by the end of this period the total amount paid out in unemployment benefit had risen to almost £1.5 billion *per annum* (it had been just £214 million in 1974), while the cost of retirement pensions (£3.6 billion when Heath went out of office) stood at £14.7 billion. Between the commencement of Harold Wilson's 1974 government and the Conservative victory of 1983 the number of people claiming and receiving supplementary benefit rose from under one million to almost 2.7 million; the cost to the Exchequer increased by a staggering 564 per cent! Put another way, when Mrs Thatcher commenced her second term as Prime Minister, about one-third of all public spending was being channelled into social-security payments of one sort or another.

In purely monetarist terms there was an immediate attraction in drastically reducing this sort of spending. But the ultimate aim of Thatcherite social policy has not been simply to save money. It is now a centrepiece of Conservative thinking that the welfare state impedes national development; individualism, self-reliance and family and communal self-help (expressed primarily through private charity) have been suppressed by a collective social provision that discounts thrift, discourages work and promotes laziness. Those who 'live off the state' (it is argued) are nothing but its slaves. To reverse this trend it is necessary to restrict this provision to the very poor; the welfare state will thus be, and come to be regarded, as an option of the last resort, as 'outdoor relief' and the workhouse were 150 years ago. A further consideration of the first importance has been that to pitch unemployment and related benefits at a level calculated to maintain a reasonable standard of living will provide the capitalist state with all the disadvantages of an army of unemployed (whose conditions of life must be kept at this level out of taxation) without any of the advantages (above all, the existence of a reservoir of cheap labour, useful in itself but also as a stick with which to beat the trade unions); the unemployed must certainly be kept from starvation, but they must not be kept very far from the thought of it.

In the early years of Thatcherite rule the obvious popularity of the welfare state acted as a brake against the implementation of these philosophies in full. Indeed, because of the then existing policy of linking pension increases to forecasts of future inflation, the real value of pensions increased by 7 per cent between November 1978 and November 1982, and the real value of some other welfare benefits, such as mobility and attendance allowances and family income supplement, also increased; the education and housing budgets were cut, but unemployment-benefit payouts continued to rise. Some tentative steps were, however, taken to reduce the real value of other benefits. Until November 1980 child benefit was frozen at its May 1979 value. In 1980 the level of a variety of benefits, including those paid to the unemployed and the sick, was raised by 5 per cent less than the rate of inflation; this 'abatement' was restored in November 1983, but at the same time the benefits were made liable to tax.

The 1980 budget reduced benefits to the families of strikers by £12 a week, while short-term benefits payable to the sick, the unemployed and the disabled were cut by 5 per cent in real terms. In 1981 the government brought to an end the system by which the value of unemployment and other long-term benefits had been linked to movements in prices or earnings (whichever yielded the bigger increase), and linked them henceforth to prices alone; in the financial year 1982–3 this saved about £500 million. In January 1982 the earnings-related supplements to unemployment, sickness, injury, maternity and widows' benefits were abolished — though earnings-related National Insurance contributions continued to be levied. In 1983 the government announced that pensions would in future be increased by reference to the actual increase in inflation over the previous twelve months, rather than to a forecast of the likely future increase. We might also note that around these major contractions there was a series of secondary — but, for those affected by them, none the less serious — reversals of policy, such as the withdrawal from students of the right to claim supplementary benefit during vacations and the shifting of responsibility for the payment of the first eight weeks of sickness benefit from the state to the employers.

All in all, by the end of its first term in office the government reckoned it had saved £2 billion a year from the social-security budget. Some of this saving had been used to finance a cut in the standard rate of income tax. Real spending on the welfare state increased during this period, but only by about 2 per cent — much less than was needed to maintain, let alone improve, the existing level of provision. During Mrs Thatcher's second term the position materially worsened. The government's own figures show that between 1979 and 1986 spending on the National Health Service increased by an average of just 2.5 per cent *per annum*—much less than the rate of inflation, while spending on social security rose by an annual average of about 4.2 per cent—that is, it just about kept pace with inflation.

In relation to real social needs the welfare state has been attacked, therefore, in two ways. First, government spending on personal social services and the NHS has not matched demands. It is true that spending on the NHS overall has been maintained in real terms at an average rate of growth of about 3 per cent *per annum*, and that the number of doctors, dentists, nurses and midwives has increased. But it has to be remembered that at least half that annual growth of 3 per cent is needed merely to maintain the existing level of provision (especially for the growing number of elderly people requiring care), and as a contribution towards medical research. The substantial and long-overdue pay rises pledged to nurses in April 1988 were, exceptionally, met by the Treasury in full; but, in general, Area Health Authorities have had to fund wage increases out of existing budgets. In real *net* terms, after taking these factors into account, spending on the NHS has grown by only about 1 per cent *per annum* since 1979; in the period 1981 to 1987 there has, indeed, been a cumulative shortfall of £600 million in hospital provision. Because it has refused to sanction significant increases in spending to produce additional resources, the government has been reduced to unpopular expedients, such as encouraging the contracting-out of cleaning, catering and laundry services, limiting the range of drugs and medicines available to NHS patients and imposing very substantial increases in charges for prescriptions and optical and dental treatment, including the ending of free eye and dental check-ups.

Secondly, and consequentially, people have been told to look to private provision, if they can, to make good the deficiencies of the state system: hospitals have been encouraged to apply to private charities to obtain extra funding; private 'pay' beds have been reintroduced into the NHS; in 1982 income-tax relief was restored for those earning up to £8,500 a year and participating in employer-employee medical insurance schemes. There has been a modest growth in the number of subscribers to private health insurance schemes overall, and co-operation between the NHS and private medicine (for example, in the use of expensive equipment) has been encouraged. On the education front it is planned to introduce student loans, while the Assisted Places Scheme has whetted the appetite of working- and lower-middle-class parents for private education as an alternative to a state system widely recognised to be grossly under-funded. The 1988 Education Act allows local authorities to charge parents for a limited range of educational services (for example, field-trips) hitherto provided free within the state system.

Until 1987 the major factor restraining the government from mounting a frontal assault on the welfare state was the undoubted odium that would be incurred thereby. No one knew how widespread this odium would be, and how much damage it might do in electoral terms. It could not, certainly, be carried out during the government's first term; the plans were not ready and, in any case, there were other priorities. None the less some tentative steps were taken to this end. Ferdinand Mount, political editor of the *Spectator*, was appointed by Mrs Thatcher to head her Downing Street Policy Unit. He brought together a committee of Cabinet Ministers, known as the Family Policy Group, charged with the task of identifying and seeking ways of counteracting 'those factors which tend to undermine, or even prohibit, the exercise of personal responsibility and a sense of individual self-respect'.[5] Some of the outpourings of this group were leaked in the *Guardian* in March 1983; its proposals included education vouchers, greater incentives for mothers to remain at home (thus creating job opportunities for males) and an overall reduction in the part played by the welfare state in the life of the nation. Elderly people, one discussion document argued, should be helped by their families 'to live full and happy lives . . . with minimum dependence upon the state'; social needs should be provided by private business and charitable services wherever possible; the welfare state should offer merely a basic minimum, a safety-net for those genuinely unable to obtain help elsewhere.

These conclusions were complemented by those of the Central Policy Review Staff, which had been asked to examine ways of reducing public spending. In answer to this question the CPRS put before the Cabinet a number of startling proposals, including the ending of direct state funding of education and a shift to private health insurance (including a minimum compulsory element) to cover the major areas of social-service provision; in effect, the suggestion was that the welfare state be privatised, leaving the government with the obligation merely to pay a very limited number of benefits on a strict means-tested basis.

At the time (1982) these ideas were regarded by the Cabinet as unacceptable, and (not without some persuasion) Mrs Thatcher agreed not to proceed with them. Some Cabinet ministers argued that they represented a definitive break with One Nation Toryism; others that, however desirable the ideas might be, it would be politically suicidal to introduce them at a time when support for more spending on the NHS (even if this meant lower or even no tax cuts) was growing. A Gallup poll conducted in July 1983 revealed that half the respondents felt government spending on the social services was already too low. So the options put forward by the CPRS and the Family Policy Unit were shelved. But they were not forgotten. Once the 1983 election had been got out of the way, the plans were resurrected, and entrusted to the care of a Cabinet much less squeamish about their implementation.

The composition of the Thatcher government of 1983–7 differed significantly from that of 1979–83. In 1979 Mrs Thatcher had been obliged to include in the Cabinet a large number of 'Heathites'; 18 of the 22 members of the her first Cabinet had served under Heath, and only a handful, such as Geoffrey Howe (Exchequer), Keith Joseph (Industry) and Patrick Jenkin (Social Services), could be regarded as personal supporters and convinced monetarists. During the term of office of this first administration the balance of power in the Cabinet was slowly turned in a Thatcherite direction. In 1981 a number of 'wets' (Ian Gilmour, Mark Carlisle and Lord Soames) were dismissed, while Lord Thorneycroft was relieved of his post as Chairman of the party. The vacancies thus created enabled the Prime Minister to promote politicians whose background and/or outlook (lower-middle-class, non-aristocratic, self-made business and professional people) matched her own; the appointments included that of Norman Tebbit, the son of an East London shop manager, at the Department of Employment; Cecil Parkinson, whose father had been a railwayman, as the new party Chairman with a seat in the Cabinet as Paymaster-General; Norman Fowler was put in charge of Social Services, Keith Joseph was moved to Education while another monetarist, Nicholas Ridley, became Financial Secretary to the Treasury.

After the 1983 election this bloc of loyal Thatcherites, trained in the legal professions and in business, and without the sort of paternalistic landowning connections that had once been the hallmark of post-war Conservative administrations, was strengthened still further; Geoffrey Howe was promoted to the Foreign Office and another monetarist hardliner, Nigel Lawson, moved to the Exchequer. The loss of Cecil Parkinson, who was obliged to seek a temporary exile from the government benches in October 1983 following news of an extra-marital relationship (and a child conceived out of wedlock), was made good a year later by the appointment, as an unpaid minister without portfolio, of David Young, who had been in charge of the Manpower Services Commission since 1982. Young had never been in Parliament. He was given a life peerage and a seat in the Cabinet, charged with responsibility for small businesses, job creation and the deregulation of industry. The promotion brought to four the number of Jews in the Cabinet, a reflection of the entrepreneurial tone of Mrs Thatcher's second administration.

These developments at Cabinet level were complemented by significant changes in the composition of the Conservative parliamentary party. As Table 5.1 indicates, the number of Conservative MPs educated at secondary school only has increased since 1979, and indeed since 1964 (see Table 4.1), while the number educated

Table 5.1 Education and occupation of Conservative MPs, 1979–1987

	1979	1983	1987
Secondary and university	55	71	69
Public school only	68	67	41
Public school and university	178	211	194
Professions	111	132	110
Armed services	20	18	15
Teachers	18	20	25
Business	115	142	139

Source: adapted from D. Butler & D. Kavanagh, *The British General Election of 1979* (Macmillan, 1980), *The British General Election of 1983* (Macmillan, 1984) and *The British General Election of 1987* (Macmillan, 1988).

at public school only has decreased. In the Parliament of 1974–9 less than 100 Conservative backbenchers came from the world of business; by 1983 the number had increased to 142.

Thus fortified, the Cabinet, in the context of a renewed onslaught against the level of public spending, made another attempt to contract the size and limit the scope of the welfare state. In March 1984 a Treasury Green Paper, *The Next Ten Years: Public Expenditure and Taxation into the 1990s*, pointed out that further tax cuts depended on a reduction in spending. The Treasury did not, at that time, offer any hostages to fortune, but a major preoccupation behind its spending policies was to reduce the role of government—directly and indirectly—in the provision of housing, through retrenchment in the programme to build new houses, in housing improvement grants and in housing benefit. The following year Norman Fowler initiated a fundamental review of four core elements of the welfare state: housing benefit, supplementary benefits, child benefit and pensions. The results of these deliberations were published (June 1985) in another Green Paper, *The Reform of Social Security*.

The Fowler Green Paper revealed, for the first time, the extent of the attack on the welfare state that was now being proposed. While acknowledging that there were groups and individuals in society whose deprivation was real, and whose needs were genuine, Fowler indicated that in the government's view these claims would have to be subordinated to wider considerations of economic strategy. Whether or not the cost of the welfare state *could* be met by direct taxation (in the form both of income tax and national insurance contributions), the objective of reducing such taxation was paramount. In consequence, the welfare state would have to be slimmed down. Reductions in housing benefit would save £500 million a year. The admittedly over-complicated schemes of supplementary benefits would be superseded by a form of income support that would be cash-limited. The flat-rate child benefit, paid to mothers regardless of their poverty or wealth, would be retained but its value would be deliberately allowed to fall in real terms.

Finally, the Green Paper addressed the matter of the State Earnings Related Pension Scheme (SERPS). SERPS, inaugurated in the late 1970s by the Labour government but with official Conservative support, was the final expression of the politics of consensus. It provided those (mainly the lower paid) who did not have available to them an approved employer-provided earnings-related pension scheme with the opportunity to participate in a state-run scheme that would give a pension, in addition to the established flat-rate pension, based on the 20 best years' earnings of the contributor. The reform was, to a modest degree, egalitarian in intent, but it offended Thatcherite principles in a number of ways. First, its success depended upon the ability to meet current liabilities out of current contributions; while the number of pensioners was due to fall in the 1990s, it would rise after the first decade of the twenty-first century, thus placing an increased burden on the taxpayer. Secondly, SERPS elevated the status of the central government as a provider of social security; it was possible to 'contract out' of the scheme, but Thatcherism preferred a system whereby individuals would be obliged to make their own pension arrangements in the private sector. The Green Paper accordingly suggested that SERPS be shut down over a period of three years; later (in a White Paper published in December 1985) it was announced that SERPS would be reprieved, but only in a form (offering a pension based on one-fifth of earnings, rather than one quarter) that was bound to make it much less attractive.

Enacted in 1986, what is undoubtedly the most thorough-going reform of the social-security system to be undertaken in Britain since the late 1940s came into effect in April 1988. What is its overall impact? Supplementary Benefit has been replaced by Income Support, a relatively simple means-tested benefit restricted to those working for no more than 24 hours a week (rather than 30 hours as hitherto). People with savings of £3,000 did not qualify for Supplementary Benefit; the limit has now been raised to £8,000, but for each £250, or part thereof, over £3,000 held in the form of capital (excluding home and personal possessions) there will be a reduction of £1 per week in Income Support, even if the savings are in the form of Premium Bonds, which do not necessarily generate any income at all. A number of 'Premiums', in addition to Income Support, are payable to particular categories of claimant, such as the disabled. People receiving Income Support may also be entitled to help with housing costs, but not for water rates, house maintenance and insurance; from January 1987 mortgage interest payments advanced by the state to those under 60 has been limited to not more than half the amount due, nor are these payments continued for more than 16 weeks. Even the poorest will have to pay 20 per cent of the rates due on the homes they occupy.

The second element in the new regime is Family Credit, which supplements the wages of low-paid workers and replaces and is more generous than Family Income Supplement, since eligibility is based on net rather than on gross income. But the munificence encountered here has been more than offset by the most controversial part of the reformed system, the Social Fund. In the past the poor were entitled to single ('one-off') payments for certain items, such as clothing and household goods. Until August 1986 the total amount paid for such purchases was about £400 million. Now (1988–9) there will be a cash limit of £203 million on the Fund, only £60 million of which will be available as outright grants; the rest will be paid as loans repayable over periods not exceeding 18 months. Grants and loans will be paid principally to families with children; but loans will only be permitted to those who can prove they can afford the repayments. Even if a claimant is able to furnish such evidence, the local social-security office may have run out of its monthly allocation; in that case, the claim will be refused, and cannot be resubmitted for another six months, no matter how great the need. In assessing entitlement to a Social Fund payment, local officers must also have regard to other sources of possible finance —in other words, private charitable foundations, to which claimants otherwise refused will in any case have to turn.

In the nineteenth century public provision of relief for the needy was based on a system of meagre out-door relief (cash payments) and board and lodging in workhouses, the condition of which was made as repulsive and degrading as possible, to act as a deterrent; the poor were obliged to turn to charities if they wished to avoid this fate. What the Thatcherite reform of the welfare state has done is to hasten a return to a state of affairs in which the major part in the relief of poverty is played by charitable institutions. Welfare provision—in short—is being privatised.

By the government's own admission, about eight million people in Britain will be affected by these new arrangements—almost three times the number classed as poor in 1979. Some will undoubtedly be better off. Many—perhaps most—will not. Quite apart from reductions in the real value of benefits still payable, there have been very substantial reductions in the numbers receiving sickness benefit and free school meals; the link between pensions and earnings has, as we have seen, been removed, the real value of child benefit has been allowed to fall, personal social services have contracted and prescription charges have risen (by 500 per cent since 1979).

In the House of Commons in 1988 Mrs Thatcher insisted that only 12 per cent of those on social security would be worse off. But Department of Health & Social Security figures suggest that the proportion is nearer 35 per cent, a survey by the independent Policy Studies Unit has put the figure at 48 per cent, while research at Oxford University has concluded that no less than 77 per cent of claimants will be adversely affected by the new system. The government's own Social Security Advisory Committee (Sixth Report, 1988) has pointed to the fact that for many of the young, the low paid and the poor there will be real additional hardship, arising particularly through adverse changes in the scope of housing benefit and the replacement of grants by loans. Additionally, in a quite separate move also implemented in the spring of 1988, benefit payable to the long-term unemployed is being refused where an applicant declines to visit a job club.

Clearly, the extent of the additional hardship will depend on the take-up rate of loans from the Social Fund. The idea that those already judged poor enough to receive Income Support will be in a position to repay loans to the Social Fund does indeed seem far-fetched. The alleged aim of this new arrangement is to restore to the poor a sense of financial responsibility and self-respect. 'What we are saying [Social Services Secretary John Moore has argued] is that those on benefit cannot and should not be shielded from shouldering the normal responsibilities which all other families face.'[6] It seems doubtful, however, whether the genuinely poor will read this lesson into the situation that now faces them. To target the welfare state on those in real need, to stamp out fraud and to prosecute and punish those who abuse the system is both fair and necessary. But to tell the unemployed and the low-paid that their legitimate needs cannot be met because the Social Fund is cash-limited would only be above criticism if the Exchequer really did not have the resources to relieve their poverty.

This is, of course, very far from being the case. While £220 million extra has been provided for Income Support, and £225 million extra for Family Credit, no less than £640 million has been saved on housing benefit, £120 million on child benefit and £230 million by the introduction of the Social Fund—a net saving of £545 million on the 1988–9 social-security budget. This money has been redistributed to the rich.

In his budget of 1988 the Chancellor, Nigel Lawson, carried out a sweeping reform of the tax system. The standard rate of income tax was reduced from 27 to 25 per cent, while all rates above the next highest rate (40 per cent on incomes above £19,300) were abolished. The top 5 per cent of taxpayers thus had their tax burden reduced by £2,690 million, and the top 10 per cent by £3,160 million; a married man on average earnings will have benefited to the extent of just £253.76 *per annum*. When the Conservatives came to power in 1979 the standard rate of income tax was 33 per cent, and the top rate on earned income stood at 83 per cent. By raising personal allowances (which have increased by a quarter, in real terms, under Mrs Thatcher) by about twice the percentage needed to keep pace with inflation, and by reducing the impact of direct taxation, Mr Lawson was able to produce a package of tax cuts totalling nearly £4 billion.

Where has this money come from? In part, from higher tax revenues (derived especially from corporation tax and VAT returns boosted by a credit-financed consumer-spending boom). In part from the sale of nationalised industries (which has yielded some £12.8 billion to the Treasury since 1979). And in part from the contraction of the welfare state. This contraction has not been effected without protest. In the winter of 1987–8 the government had to make an emergency injection of £100 million into the National Health Service to meet public criticism, and in April 1988 the Treasury was obliged to produce £750 million from the contingency reserve to fund pay awards for the doctors and the nurses. However, it is the view of Downing Street that further funding for the NHS must be found from internal savings, such as more efficient use of resources and the sale of surplus land. For the foreseeable future, it seems, the Conservative nation will encompass a welfare state, but it will be much smaller and able to give only a restricted service.

The Public Sector Borrowing Requirement, which stood at 1 per cent of Gross Domestic Product in 1987–8, is now set at zero for the rest of the government's third term in office. This does indeed represent a balanced budget—a long-held Thatcherite dream come true. It means, however, that while the prosperous will be allowed to prosper, the poor will be increasingly expected to help themselves. It is a fundamental tenet of Thatcherism that very substantial inequalities of wealth are necessary in British society in order to foster enterprise and stimulate growth.[7] That is to say, greed and envy will spur the less well-off to emulate their more prosperous fellow citizens, thus setting in motion a process that will improve national economic performance. Some Conservatives argue that, as a result, more revenue will flow into the Treasury, to be used, prudently, to strengthen the welfare state. But the truth is that by the end of the century there will be much less of a welfare state left to strengthen.

Thatcherism has been represented to the electorate as a liberating creed, a set of policies designed to 'roll back' the state and to give people more control over their own lives. In some respects it has done just this. The sale of council houses has been so popular that it is unlikely any future government will compulsorily order their repurchase. The privatisation programme has not returned nationalised industries 'to the people', as the 1987 Tory Manifesto claimed; a member of the public who acquired shares in this way, and who did not sell them at once for a modest but quick profit, has a say in British Telecom, or British Gas, so small that it is hardly worth turning up to the annual mass meetings of shareholders. Privatisation has, in practice, given managements a much greater freedom to manage without let or hindrance. At the same time privatisation has undoubtedly introduced the concept of share ownership to many who would otherwise have remained ignorant of it. In 1979 there were less than 3 million shareholders in Britain; now they number about 9.5 million. The selling-off of state-run enterprises, taken together with deregulation of industry, the abolition of many restrictions with which small businesses have had to contend hitherto in the fields of employment and planning, and the outlawing of monopolistic practices in areas such as house conveyancing and the supply of telephone equipment, have contributed to an atmosphere much more conducive to private enterprise and competition. Certainly in terms of service to the public, the expectations of customers and consumers have risen; standards ought to rise as a result.

But in some crucial areas of national activity the sphere of the state has been extended dramatically. Local authorities are now bound hand and foot to Whitehall, so much so that freedoms which they enjoyed have been taken away literally overnight. On 8 March 1988 Environment Secretary Nicholas Ridley announced that he would be using powers given in the Prescribed Expenditure Regulations to outlaw, from midnight, the perfectly legal practice of local authorities raising money through the sale and leaseback of buildings; in relation to one such transaction, already entered into by the London Borough of Brent, Mr Ridley went so far as to express 'regret' that what had been done, by an elected authority, was within the law.

In the field of education reform the same contempt for the views of those affected by proposed changes can been seen at work. Kenneth Baker's decision in February 1988 to dismantle (with effect from 1990) the Inner London Education Authority, a proposal which had never been placed before the electorate and which, on survey evidence, is opposed by a majority of Inner London parents, is a case in point. The initial proposal to exclude religious education from the National Curriculum is another. The National Curriculum itself represents a centralisation of authority on a scale as yet unknown in modern Britain, and the new funding arrangements for universities and polytechnics mean that these institutions of higher education will no longer be free to teach subjects of which the government of the day disapproves.

These authoritarian tendencies may be observed not only in specific areas of government policy, but—more disturbingly—in the way the actual process of government has been carried out since 1979. This is the facet of Thatcherism that is least obvious to the generality of voters, but most fundamental to an understanding of the nature of Mrs Thatcher's rule. In a celebrated interview with Kenneth Harris in the *Observer* of 25 February 1979 she announced her intention not to 'waste time having any internal arguments' were she to become Prime Minister. We know, of course (not least from the information that became public during the Westland affair, in the winter of 1985–6) that Cabinet meetings under Margaret Thatcher are lively, not to say heated. None the less, under Mrs Thatcher a subtle change has taken place in the balance of authority as between the full Cabinet and the office of Prime Minister.

The quality of Cabinet government in Britain depends very much upon the personality and intentions of the Cabinet chairman, the Prime Minister. As the victor in three successive general elections Mrs Thatcher's authority, in the Cabinet, no less than in the party she leads, was bound to have grown. She has taken advantage of this authority over the past decade to remove from the Cabinet those whose views and outlook she perceives as unreliable in relation to the policies she has wished to pursue; the Cabinet now consists largely of ministers who owe their position to her alone, rather than to their own standing within the parliamentary party. This, too, is to some extent an inevitable result of her long tenure of office. Her dismissal of ministers in 1981 has been portrayed as brutal; but it does not bear comparison with the sackings which Harold Macmillan carried out in July 1962, when seven Cabinet ministers, including some of his most loyal supporters, were dismissed.

Mrs Thatcher has preserved the form of Cabinet government. But she has carried out a fundamental alteration in its substance, with the object of denying to fellow members of the Cabinet the resources with which to challenge her interpretation of policy. An early step in this direction, hardly commented upon by the media at the time, was her decision in 1979 to reduce from two to one the number of paid political advisers each Cabinet minister might appoint. The Central Policy Review Staff that Heath had established in 1970 to advise the Cabinet as a whole on policy initiatives was abolished in 1983; this has left the Policy Unit—*her* Policy Unit—as the major provider of briefs for Cabinet consideration. She has brought into Downing Street her own political aides (such as the economist Sir Alan Walters and the diplomat Sir Anthony Parsons) to counter the inertia or timidity of the career Civil

Service (in these examples the Treasury and the Foreign Office) and she has displayed more than a passing interest in the appointment of top civil servants, especially Permanent Secretaries: for example, Clive Whitmore, her principal private secretary, to the Ministry of Defence and the monetarist Peter Middleton to the Treasury (both 1983). The Civil Service Department has been wound up, and the Civil Service has once more been placed under the direct control of the Treasury.

Most significant of all, Mrs Thatcher has downgraded the role of the full Cabinet in the discussion and formulation of national policy. First, she has reduced the number of Cabinet meetings from an average of two per week to less than one; Cabinets meet less frequently and the amount of information given to members, in the form of Cabinet Papers, is now much reduced (not more than about 70 a year, one-sixth of the number tabled in the 1950s). Secondly, she has deliberately steered the discussion of sensitive matters away from the full Cabinet, and even from Cabinet committees, into informal meetings of ministers and senior advisers. It was in this way, for example, that the decision to ban trade unions at GCHQ was taken in 1984 by a small group (initially the Prime Minister, the Foreign Secretary and the Defence Secretary) quite outside the formal Cabinet structure; the decision to allow President Reagan the use of British bases from which to carry out a bombing raid on Libya (April 1986) was, likewise, taken by an *ad hoc* group.

Thirdly, even in her conduct of the business of the full Cabinet, Mrs Thatcher has become strident, domineering and intolerant of the views of others. It is worth recalling that what turned the arguments about the future of the Westland helicopter company from a dispute into an affair was the Prime Minister's decision to cancel a special Cabinet meeting scheduled for 13 December to discuss the rival American and European bids to take over the Westland concern; Mrs Thatcher's refusal to allow Defence Secretary Michael Heseltine to raise the matter at a routine Cabinet on 12 December; her determination not to have Mr Heseltine's comments recorded in the Cabinet minutes, and her demand (put to him at a Cabinet held on 9 January 1986) that all future ministerial statements on Westland be cleared with the Cabinet Office.

Mr Heseltine's critics were right to point out that constitutional government was not at stake. Mrs Thatcher could have been overruled, in her treatment of him, by the full Cabinet; it was he, not they, who resigned. However, to say this is not to acquit Mrs Thatcher of the charge of authoritarianism, but rather to include those in government who owe their positions to her, and who are loyal to her, of complicity in the promotion of it. The obsessional determination to spend as much as it cost trying to prevent Peter

Wright from publishing his memoirs, the pressure brought on BBC Television in August 1985 not to show the programme 'Real Lives' (about the IRA), and on both the BBC and the IBA in April 1988 over the screening of television programmes (however controversial) on the shooting of IRA terrorists in Gibraltar, do not inspire confidence in the commitment of Mrs Thatcher's administration to the tenets of an open society. Three election victories seem to have convinced the Thatcherites that a government of conviction (in itself no bad thing) is incompatible with government by consent. A fourth term in office is likely to strengthen the view that whatever Mrs Thatcher thinks must, by that fact alone, be right.

NOTES

1. In S. Hall & M. Jacques (eds., 1983), *The Politics of Thatcherism*, London, Lawrence & Wishart, p. 113.
2. This was pointed out as early as 1946 by Professor H. Finer (*The Road to Reaction*), who prophesied correctly that Hayek's programme could only be carried out 'through a massive accretion of power at the centre'.
3. Quoted in D. Kavanagh (1987), *Thatcherism and British Politics*, London, Macmillan, p. 105.
4. See I. Gough, 'Thatcherism and the Welfare State', in Hall and Jacques, *The Politics of Thatcherism*, p. 149.
5. Central Policy Review Staff, Note to Ministers, September 1982.
6. *Observer*, 10 April 1988.
7. Norman Tebbit (who retired to the backbenches after the 1987 general election) made this candid admission in an interview with Vivian White on BBC Television, 8 May 1988.

6. A One-Party State?

Although, under a succession of Conservative governments since 1979, British society has become more divided, and the inequalities of wealth and poverty more stark, those whom the policies of Thatcherite Conservatism have favoured have undoubtedly done very well. Post-war British governments are generally evaluated by their performance in managing the economy. Judged on this basis, Mrs Thatcher's administrations have fulfilled their promise.

The government's overriding priority since coming into office has been to reduce inflation, which averaged nearly 14 per cent *per annum* between 1971 and 1980. In recent years it has fallen to between 3 and 7.5 per cent. Economists argue about the extent to which the government itself can take credit for this trend. It is generally acknowledged that since 1979 the Treasury has consistently failed to meet its own monetary targets—that is, to reduce the money supply to a pre-set level. High interest rates have helped to bolster and maintain the strength of sterling, which has assisted the fight against inflation. So has the slowing down of the rate of wage increases, in which the growth in unemployment levels has certainly played a part; registered unemployment reached a record 11.1 per cent of the workforce at the beginning of 1987, and has only recently begun to fall. However, just as the great inflation of the 1970s had been fuelled by increases in world commodity prices, so the fall in such prices in the 1980s has had the opposite effect; for this, of course, the government deserves neither blame nor praise.

Another Conservative preoccupation has been to contain and if possible reduce public spending. But during the lifetime of the government this has only begun to happen very recently; as a proportion of the Gross National Product, only in 1986 did this percentage (43.3 per cent) fall below the 1979 level (43.5 per cent). The Public Sector Borrowing Requirement has fallen (as we noted in the previous chapter) from 5.5 per cent of GNP in 1980 to zero in 1988. But until 1988 this reduction has been achieved artificially, through the sale of council houses and the massive privatisation programme. The contraction of the welfare state will undoubtedly assist the policy of maintaining the PSBR at zero; this process will be greatly assisted if (as some Tories are now arguing) people are allowed to opt out of the National Health Service altogether, and if the government succeeds in its policy of selling off all council houses by converting rents into inflation-linked mortgage payments.

In terms of national popularity, however, the fact that Mrs Thatcher happened to occupy 10 Downing Street at a time when inflation was likely to fall, and during a period when the PSBR contracted artificially is not very important. Most voters are only dimly aware of the meaning of the PSBR and the GNP. What matters to them is the quality of their lives, the size of their wage packets or salary cheques, the degree of stability in the economy and (hence) in society, and the international standing of the country in which they live. For those out of work—particularly those in middle or later life, when retraining is a daunting experience to contemplate, the Thatcher years have on the whole been profoundly unhappy ones; we can understand it if they blame the Conservatives for their lot in life, although the numbers of unemployed voting Conservative (see Chapter One) suggest that they are by no means undiscriminating. For those in work, however, the Thatcher years have amounted to a golden age.

Leaving aside entirely the price (pre-eminently as reflected in unemployment and restrictions on the freedom of trade unions) that has been paid, there is no denying the fact that Britain has become more prosperous during the 1980s, both absolutely and in comparison with other economies. Between 1979 and 1987 Britain's Gross Domestic Product increased by 15.5 per cent; French GDP rose by 13.9 per cent and that of West Germany by 11.4 per cent. Between 1983 and 1987 the French economy grew by about 7 per cent, the West German by just over 9 per cent, but the British by over 14 per cent.

By this measure, Britain's economic growth rate is now higher than that of West Germany, Japan or the USA; in 1984 it was the lowest of the four. Investment by British companies in plant and machinery is ahead of that to be found in Germany or Japan; partly as a consequence, British productivity is on the increase. Measured in terms of Gross Domestic Product per hour worked, the productivity of the British worker began to recover in 1980; the average annual rate of increase is now of the order of 6 per cent—higher than that to be found in Japan and not far behind those of the USA and West Germany, both of which are now falling. The pre-tax profits of the British manufacturing sector fell to below 5 per cent between 1979 and 1983, but are now back to the level of the late 1960s (around 10 per cent) and are still rising.

The result has been that for those in work average weekly earnings have increased by about a third since the election of 1983, while retail prices have risen by only about a fifth—a 14 per cent increase in real disposable income. Very little of the credit for this is now given to the old confrontational style of the trade unions. Trade-union membership has fallen from 54 per cent of Britain's workforce in 1979 to 40 per cent. The nature of trade unionism has also changed. Whatever view one takes of the motives behind the Employment Acts of 1980 and 1982 and the Trade Union Act of 1984, their impact upon the incidence of strike activity cannot be doubted; employers have taken advantage of the ease with which they can now obtain injunctions, especially over secondary actions; the liability (under the 1982 Act) which trade unions must now shoulder for the actions of their shop stewards has been particularly severe.

The defeat of the National Union of Mineworkers in the year-long strike of 1984–5 over pit closures, and the failure (1986–7) of the printworkers to prevent the opening of new headquarters for the News International group of newspapers at Wapping (using computer technology operated by electricians) demonstrated the effectiveness of Conservative trade-union legislation, and helped to bring about a new climate not merely in industrial relations but in public perception of the role of trade unions in the economy. A major factor in the defeat of the NUM was the refusal of the Nottinghamshire miners to give their support; at Wapping the electricians and the lorry drivers assured Rupert Murdoch of victory. Both disputes were symptomatic of the fragmentation of the manual working classes. The TUC, which in the 1960s and 1970s was regularly consulted by governments, now finds itself on the outer fringes of the consultative process, the earliest victim of Mrs Thatcher's assault upon consensus politics and the corporate state.

Those unions which have prospered (such as the Electrical, Electronic, Telecommunications & Plumbing Union, and the Amalgamated Engineering Union) have embraced the 'new realism', which includes a willingness to enter into single-union deals with employers, and to sign no-strike agreements. In defence of these policies, the leaders of these unions point to the high wages and relative job-security enjoyed by their members, and to the fact that the alternative to their style of unionism is not the 'old unionism', but rather 'no unionism'—plants and factories in which workers are happy not to be blessed by the advantages trade unions have to offer, and still further job losses. The decision (March 1988) of Ford of America to cancel a planned £40-million electronics plant at Dundee, where unemployment was running at 15 per cent, because of the refusal of the TGWU to accept a single-union deal involving the AEU, was a dramatic illustration of the new reality, and brought a step nearer the possibility of the formation of a breakaway TUC, involving the AEU, EETPU, the Nottinghamshire-based Union of Democratic Mineworkers, and smaller professional bodies such as the National Union of Journalists.

Trade unionism has not yet been destroyed by Thatcherite Conservatism. It is worth remembering, for example, that most of the agreements by which workers have won increases in real pay have arisen out of collective bargaining. The secret voting arrangements which have been forced upon the unions have, by general consent, proved very popular; even unions with left-wing leaderships, such as the Association of Scientific, Technical & Managerial Staffs (now part of the Manufacturing, Scientific & Finance Union) have accepted government money for secret postal ballots. Mrs Thatcher has tamed the trade unions, just as she won back the Falkland Islands and forced structural changes upon the agricultural price-control arrangements of the EEC (February 1988).

Whatever the academic arguments about the true causes of Britain's prosperity since 1979, and however soundly based or merely paper-thin that prosperity might be, the weight of public opinion attributes it to the party that has enjoyed power over the past ten years. Unbridled trade-union authority is no longer an issue at the forefront of public debate. Instead, the creation and accumulation of wealth have become respectable occupations in a society that has been taught, by the Thatcherites, to respect enterprise and to suspect vested interests. Among young people, especially those who have come to maturity during the Thatcher era, a distinct 'work ethic' can be observed.[1] This climate of opinion has obvious attractions for those from working-class and middle-class backgrounds alike. Over its years in office, the Thatcher government has been highly successful in choosing as its targets for reform sectional groups that have been regarded— rightly or wrongly—as privileged and feather-bedded hitherto: the trade unions, the teachers, the universities, the nationalised industries and those who work in them, opticians, hospital consultants, solicitors, the Civil Service and (in a Green Paper published in March 1988) a host of other professional monopolies such as architects, accountants, lawyers and estate agents.

Above all, perhaps, it has been during Mrs Thatcher's tenure of

10 Downing Street that the international reputation of the United Kingdom has been restored. 'The once-sick man of Europe', the West German newspaper *Handelsblatt* wrote in March 1988, 'has become Europe's most dynamic economic nation.' This sentiment has been echoed by the quality press in Italy, France, Japan and the USA. In April 1988 the leading American business magazine, *Fortune*, announced that 'after decades of decline, the world's oldest industrial power has recovered its prowess'. According to *Fortune*, the increase in income to the British Treasury from corporate taxes in 1988, compared with 1987, will exceed the total tax revenue derived from North Sea oil. The trans-Atlantic tourist traffic, which not so many years ago flowed largely from west to east is now beginning to flow heavily also in the opposite direction, as the pound has become stronger against the dollar as well as the German mark.

Whether this new-found prosperity is real and lasting, or artificial and transitory, is a legitimate question to be asked by economists, but not by those who would understand the politics of Britain as the century draws to its close. A feeling of economic well-being has encircled the British body politic; and even if those who actually experience and embrace it comprise merely a section of the electorate, the balance of electoral forces would appear, at the moment, to give them the preponderating influence.

National self-satisfaction with Thatcherite rule, and international euphoria at its economic consequences, must not blind us to the fact that, measured against election outcomes, Conservative government is minority government; no more than any of her post-war Labour or Conservative predecessors can Mrs Thatcher claim to have the backing of the majority of the British people for the policies she pursues. Conservative support has, however, been sociologically and, to some extent, geographically reconstituted. This new electorate none the less operates within an unreformed and frankly fraudulent electoral system, of which certain features deserve special mention.

Broadly speaking, the present electoral system dates from the first half of the twentieth century; its salient features are in fact based upon the 1918 Representation of the People Act. A party which 'wins' a general election claims a mandate to enact whatever happened to have been written into its manifesto, or indeed (as with the abolition of the ILEA) whatever it feels is in the public interest as defined by it. 'Winning' a general election means, quite simply, winning a simple majority of the MPs (at present 650) in the House of Commons. These MPs, in turn, 'win' their seats by obtaining, not a majority of the votes cast in their individual constituency contests, but just the largest number of votes cast, no matter how many votes have been cast for other candidates. This, the plurality or first-past-the-post system, means that it is common

Table 6.1 Votes and seats, 1979–1987

	Votes cast (%)	Seats obtained (%)
1979		
Con	43.9	52.2
Lab	37.0	41.4
Lib	13.8	1.7
1983		
Con	42.4	61.1
Lab	27.6	32.2
All	25.4	3.5
1987		
Con	42.3	57.8
Lab	30.8	35.2
All	22.6	3.4

Table 6.2 Seats and votes in the South-East and North-West regions, 1987

Region	Seats (%)			Votes (%)		
	Con	Lab	All	Con	Lab	All
South-East	85.9	12.5	1.6	52.2	22.3	25.0
North-West	46.6	49.3	4.1	38.0	41.2	21.6

Adapted from: D. Butler & D. Kavanagh, *The British General Election of 1987* (Macmillan, 1988), p. 284.

for candidates to win seats with less than 50 per cent of the votes cast. Invariably, moreover, parties gain power even though less than half the voters choose to support them in the polling booths (see Table 6.1).

This system exaggerates the political strength of the winning party, and operates in an even more inequitable manner when more than two major parties or groupings enter the electoral contest. It is partly for this reason that the Liberal Party, and the

Table 6.3 Representation of the Alliance, Welsh and Scottish Nationalists, 1987

	Popular support	**No. of seats**
Alliance	23.8% of English votes	1.9% of English seats
Plaid Cymru	7.3% of Welsh votes	7.9% of Welsh seats
SNP	14.0% of Scottish votes	4.2% of Scottish seats

Alliance, have been systematically robbed of their true entitlement to seats at Westminster. Scarcely less serious, however, is the manner in which constituency boundaries are drawn up by the Boundary Commissions (one each for England, Wales, Scotland and Northern Ireland). Since 1958 these Commissions have not been obliged to undertake general reviews more frequently than once every ten years; and since their inception in 1944 they have never had the power to take into account *projected* population movements when redistributing seats. Very substantial differences in constituency size can in consequence develop between boundary revisions. Since the rate of population increase is slower in the North of England (where Labour did well in 1987) than in the South, this has resulted in a situation whereby the average size of constituency has tended to be smaller in the latter than in the former. In Britain in 1987 it took almost 44,000 votes to elect each Labour MP (in 1983 it had taken around 40,000), but less than 37,000 to return each Conservative MP (in 1983 around 33,000).

One particular twist of the plurality method must be stressed. The British electorate may well be split on geographical lines. The effect of the first-past-the-post system is to exaggerate this cleavage. Table 6.2 compares seats and votes in the South-East and North-West regions of England in 1987.

In the North-West (leaving aside the injustice done to the Alliance), there was a very rough correlation between seats and votes, at least to the extent that Labour's lead over the Conservatives in terms of seats won was of the same order as its lead in terms of votes cast (about 3 per cent). But in the South-East the Conservatives obtained over four-fifths of the seats for only just over half the votes.

The mechanics of the electoral system have thus acted as a distorting mirror, producing in Parliament a political chasm that appears much deeper than it is in reality. If we then add to this picture the treatment of other parties (see Table 6.3), we see that even in its treatment of minor parties the system is anything but even-handed.

Where support for a third party is territorially or culturally concentrated, the electoral system may well allow it a reasonable parliamentary representation. But if its support is more evenly spread, and more broadly based, as was the case with the Alliance, the parliamentary representation will be token only. The present electoral arrangements, in short, favour narrowly based nationalist minor parties against broadly based minor parties. We should also note that in 1987 Labour obtained 69 per cent of the Scottish seats for only 42 per cent of the Scottish votes, and 63 per cent of the Welsh seats with the support of only 45 per cent of Welsh voters.

Mrs Thatcher is clearly in a position to ignore the nationalist vote in Scotland and Wales; she has already demonstrated, through her rejection of 'Loyalist' opposition to the Anglo–Irish Agreement (giving the Republic of Ireland a voice in the government of Northern Ireland) that she is prepared to turn a blind eye to the majority view in that province, while at the same time rejecting the more extreme claims of Catholic Nationalists. Within the United Kingdom as a whole it is only the Labour Party with which she need concern herself. At the moment the signs are that, even here, her concern does not need to be very deep.

In the past, governing parties have traditionally experienced a falling-off in public support in mid-term. The available evidence at the time of writing does not suggest that this is happening to a critical extent. At the local elections of May 1988 it was the former Alliance vote that was squeezed between Labour and the Conservatives. The Conservatives made a very modest gain of five seats, while Labour's net gain was 104; the Democrats, and David Owen's SDP won 93 seats between them, but lost 168 others—a net loss of 75 seats.

Neil Kinnock was quick to claim that these results reflected a turning of the tide in Labour's favour. Only in Scotland, where Labour took control of three councils (including Aberdeen) and the SNP made 45 net gains, can this claim be said to have substance; Scotland's four largest cities—Edinburgh, Glasgow, Aberdeen and Dundee—are now all in Labour hands. In England, the Conservatives benefited from a slump in the number of votes given to the former Alliance parties, whose candidates sometimes fought each other; Labour made some headway in the North and the Midlands (taking control of Walsall and Wolverhampton, and making gains in Liverpool), and did well in capturing Southampton and Cambridge; but the Tories won control in Eastbourne, Bath and St Albans, and—surprisingly—Derby. If Scotland is excluded from the overall calculation, the Conservatives made a net gain of 27 seats.

One message of these results seems to be that the North–South electoral divide may be deepening. But we must bear in mind that Labour's strength in northern England is bound to be adversely affected as future boundary changes catch up with the population migration from north to south. It is also significant that most of the 3,800 seats contested in May 1988 did not change hands. A BBC computer analysis of the results found that Labour had the support of 41 per cent of the voters, the Conservatives only 38 per cent—a fall of 3 per cent since the general election. But in the May 1984 District Council elections Labour also did well; the Conservative vote also fell by 3 per cent and the party lost 100 seats. This proved to be no obstacle to the Tory victory in the general election three years later.

The most refined and qualified of electoral calculations can be upset by the unforeseen development, the banana-skin that no one spotted. However, the next general election is probably some years away. If the centre-ground of British—and especially of English—politics collapses, two-party politics will return; this will undoubtedly benefit Labour, but only to the extent of helping it to consolidate and extend support in areas and within groups (such as pensioners and council-tenants) where that support was strong in former times. Survey evidence collected since the 1987 general election indicates that the Labour and Conservative Parties are taking votes equally from the former Alliance voters in the professional and managerial categories, and that the Conservatives are actually doing better than Labour in terms of skilled manual-worker support.[2] If the centre-ground revives, of course, a true multi-party system will reappear; with a split opposition, and an unreformed electoral system, the Conservatives have nothing to fear from such a development.[3]

Political power in Britain in the 1980s and 1990s depends heavily on electoral outcomes in the South of England, where only 54 per cent of the electorate is working class and where only 21 per cent are council-tenants. Even if Neil Kinnock were to succeed in re-ordering the priorities of the Labour Party, so as to tailor its collectivist ideology to the social revolution that Britain has undergone over the past 20 years or so, it seems unlikely that the resulting mix of socialist rhetoric and social-market reality would prove credible, at least in the short term. There is, without doubt, genuine public concern about the National Health Service, education and unemployment; this must not be taken to reflect nationwide trust in Labour's ability to manage these concerns successfully.

Above all, Neil Kinnock, though a good Labour leader in the present circumstances, is not a great one; if Mrs Thatcher chooses to lead her party against him at the next general election, only an act of extreme carelessness would deprive her of a fourth term in office.

NOTES

1. MINTEL, *Youth Lifestyles 1986*, Mintel, London, 1988.
2. *The Times*, 18 April 1988.
3. This is precisely why the Richmond (Yorkshire) by-election result (23 February 1989) was such a good one for a Conservative government entering mid-term. At Richmond the Conservative majority was slashed from 19,576 to 2,634—the worst by-election result for the Conservatives since Orpington (1962). But at Orpington the Conservatives lost, whereas at Richmond a split opposition (rival Democrat and Owenite candidates) assured them of victory.

Present and the Future

To all who are concerned to see the survival and development of democratic institutions in the United Kingdom, the tenth anniversary of the Conservative election victory of 3 May 1979 presents a sombre occasion for analysis and reflection. By any standards, ten years of one-party rule is remarkable. The Conservative Party cannot claim to have, or to have had at any time over the past decade, majority support amongst either electors or voters. The short answer to the question 'why have the Conservatives been in power for so long?' is that this country is burdened with a demonstrably unfair electoral system, one almost designed to bestow power despite the popular will. The promotion of proportional representation needs, therefore, no apology. That one branch of the legislature is composed largely of hereditary peers, and that the other, although elected after a fashion, reflects in no way whatever the real wishes of the electorate, is a national disgrace. But what is more disgraceful still is that there appears to be no widespread sense of injustice at this state of affairs.

The blame for this lies ultimately with the electorate itself. It is generally the case that every country has the government it deserves. If a substantial part of the voting public were to begin to voice serious concern about the electoral system (as the Catholics of Northern Ireland did about the manner in which the Stormont government was elected in the 1960s), the politicians would be obliged to sit up and take notice. Not since the suffragette struggles at the beginning of this century has such a movement been seen in mainland Britain.

Equally, however, responsibility lies with the country's political leadership, which has failed the nation in two crucial respects. Those politicians who acknowledge the faults of the electoral system have none the less not given them the place of priority they deserve, preferring instead to indulge in scarcely relevant doctrinal quarrels and personal disputes. Those politicians who refuse to acknowledge the inequities of the electoral system (or who refuse to make such acknowledgement in public) have lost no time in manipulating the resultant situation to their own advantage, projecting and pursuing sectional aims on the grounds that these are 'in the national interest' whether or not these aims actually enjoy majority support.

Had the 1987 general election been held under a system of proportional representation (say, the Single Transferable Vote), the Conservative Party would have emerged with about 275 MPs, Labour with around 200, and the Alliance with perhaps 150. Given this projection, the overriding aim of the centre parties—the Democrats and the Owenite SDP—ought to be to campaign on the single issue of electoral reform. This is not being done. Instead, the parties of the centre are in evident disarray. At the SDP Conference in September 1988 David Owen did, to be sure, dwell at length on the need to bring about proportional representation, which is now (apparently) his 'greatest remaining ambition'.[1] In practical terms, however, the tiny party he leads is not, and is never likely to be, in a position to force either the Labour Party or the Conservatives to join this crusade.

At its 1988 Conference the rump SDP marked itself out as an anti-Thatcher party, firmly opposed to the 'upstairs, downstairs society' being created by Conservative rule. But Dr Owen's call for a coalition of opposition parties to defeat Mrs Thatcher was bound to be rejected by Labour and the Democrats. The SDP has, and will at the next general election have, very little bargaining strength. Its continued existence will be at best a minor irritant, and at worst a cause of further fragmentation in the ranks of the opposition. Dr Owen's new-found coolness towards Mrs Thatcher (whom he accused of harbouring a 'pathological dislike' for the National Health Service) may well be genuine. But in view of his support for Thatcherite causes in 1987 it is difficult to avoid the conclusion that he and the party he leads are unlikely to be taken seriously by the Labour Party whenever the next election is called.

Under Paddy Ashdown the Democrats, titular heirs to the Liberal/Alliance inheritance, have yet to establish their credibility. On being elected first leader of the Democrats (July 1988), Ashdown immediately ruled out a future pact with either the Owenites or Labour, thus continuing the tradition of political myopia that has come to be associated with the centre of British politics. 'I have made it clear', Ashdown declared, 'that the period of coalitions, necessary though it was, is now over . . . I can see no reason at all why we should now be talking about coalitions, pacts and alliances. We are on our own, and we are going to make it on our own.'

In the Britain of the 1990s 'making it on our own' can only mean replacing Labour as an alternative party of government. Mr Ashdown's ferocious onslaught against Thatcherism, his denunciation of the erosion of civil liberties over which Mrs Thatcher has presided, and his perceptive attack on her manipulation of patriotism made wonderful listening, and reading. But the decision of the Democrats to espouse the phasing out of nuclear power-stations is bound to make it suspect in the eyes of many voters, and this suspicion will be increased a thousandfold if the issue of nuclear disarmament (tactfully avoided by the Democrats in 1988) is resolved in a unilateralist direction in 1989.

The surest way in which any party in Britain can lose popular appeal is to support unilateralism. The success of multilateral arms-reduction negotiations, and the popularity of such arrangements, merely serves to underline the truth of this proposition. Unilateralism, reaffirmed by a large majority at its Blackpool Conference in October 1988, is a burden so heavy for the Labour Party to bear that it is difficult to see how any amount of verbal dexterity over 'public ownership' and 'social ownership' can be realistically offered to the electorate by way of consolation. In any case, the power wielded by the left, and especially left-wing trade unions (pre-eminently the TGWU and its unilateralist General Secretary Ron Todd) within the counsels of Labour is now so blatant that no Labour leader can with truth tell the country that he is really, and ultimately, representative of the party he leads.

The negative image which Labour-affiliated trade unions project of the Labour movement as a whole is certainly recognised within the party. The close relationship between the TUC and Labour is being questioned more urgently in the light of the expulsion from the TUC of the electricians (September 1988) and (arguably more serious) the boycott by the TUC of the government's Employment Training scheme, more especially since the decision to boycott this scheme has presented the government with a unique opportunity to deal consensus politics a further blow by bringing to an end the automatic representation of the unions on a number of public bodies, including the National Economic Development Council. The government can now plead with some justification that the Labour movement itself has attempted to undermine its efforts to deal with unemployment.

It may well be that the quite legitimate but separate interests and preoccupations of Labour and the unions have now diverged so far that, in an ideal world, it would be sensible for all concerned to bring the marriage to an end. No one can doubt that such a divorce would be exceedingly painful and, for the Labour Party, exceedingly damaging in the short and medium terms. Labour leaders were quick to explain the party's narrow failure to win the Kensington by-election (14 July 1988) as being due primarily to the damaging effect on potential Labour support of the Benn-Heffer leadership challenge. A schism between the party and its trade unions would certainly be more damaging still. And from where else would party revenue be derived?

As senior a figure in the Labour Party as Robin Cook, a member of the Shadow Cabinet and Neil Kinnock's campaign manager in the leadership contest, has already gone on record as doubting whether Labour could win an outright majority at the next general election; the most that could be hoped for (he declared) was a hung Parliament.[2] Since an anti-Conservative coalition seems to have been ruled out by both Labour and Democrat leaders, the chances are that, even against the backcloth of a parliamentary stalemate, Mrs Thatcher could easily remain at 10 Downing Street. But even the possibility of a hung Parliament seems, on present evidence, very remote.

High interest rates are unpopular with borrowers; but house-buyers and businessmen are unlikely to vote Labour simply in the hope that interest rates will come down if Mr Kinnock were Prime Minister. The relative stability that Britain has enjoyed since 1979 has been bought at a price. At three successive general elections, however, enough voters have been willing to pay it to ensure Conservative victories. Given the present electoral system, and the commitment of both Labour and Conservative parties to its retention, the best hope of bringing an end to Conservative rule is the very coalition that Neil Kinnock and Paddy Ashdown refuse to contemplate. Unless and until they—or their successors—do so, the possibility of a non-Conservative government emerging before the late 1990s seems remote indeed.

NOTES

1. *The Times*, 19 September 1988.
2. *The Times*, 20 August 1988.

Further Reading

CHAPTER ONE

D. Butler & D. Kavanagh, *The British General Election of 1987* (Macmillan, London, 1988)

A. Heath, R. Jowell & J. Curtice, *How Britain Votes* (Pergamon Press,
Oxford, 1985)

D. Robertson, *Class and the British Electorate* (Basil Blackwell, Oxford, 1984)

CHAPTER TWO

D. Kavanagh (ed.), *The Politics of the Labour Party* (Allen & Unwin, London, 1982)

D. & M. Kogan, *The Battle for the Labour Party* (Fontana, London, 1982)

A. Mitchell, *Four Years in the Death of the Labour Party* (Methuen, London, 1983)

CHAPTER THREE

V. Bogdanov (ed.), *Liberal Party Politics* (Clarendon Press, Oxford, 1983)

I. Bradley, *Breaking the Mould? The Birth and Prospects of The Social Democratic Party* (Martin Robertson, Oxford, 1981)

I. Bradley (ed.), *The Strange Rebirth of Liberal Britain* (Chatto & Windus, London, 1985)

CHAPTER FOUR

R. Blake, *The Conservative Party from Disraeli to Thatcher* (Fontana, London, 1985)

A. Gamble, *The Conservative Nation* (Routledge & Kegan Paul, London, 1974)

Z. Layton-Henry (ed.), *Conservative Party Politics* (Macmillan, London, 1980)

CHAPTER FIVE

S. Hall & M. Jacques (eds.), *The Politics of Thatcherism* (Lawrence & Wishart, London, 1983)

D. Kavanagh, *Thatcherism and British Politics: The End of Consensus?* (Oxford University Press, Oxford, 1987)

P. Riddell, *The Thatcher Government*, 2nd edn (Basil Blackwell, Oxford, 1985)

CHAPTER SIX

S. Ingle, *The British Party System* (Basil Blackwell, Oxford, 1987)

G. Thompson, *The Conservative Economic Policy* (Croom Helm, London, 1986)

A. Walters, *Britain's Economic Renaissance: Margaret Thatcher's Economic Reforms, 1979–1984* (Oxford University Press, Oxford, 1985)

Index